SPRINTS AND RELAYS
Contemporary Theory, Technique and Training

Third Edition

EDITED BY JESS JARVER

TAFNEWS PRESS

Book Division of Track & Field News

First published in 1990 by Tafnews Press,
Book Division of Track & Field News,
2570 El Camino Real, Suite 606,
Mountain View, CA 94040 USA.

Copyright © 1990 by Tafnews Press

First edition printed in 1978
Second edition printed in 1983
Third edition, with all-new material, printed in 1990

Standard Book Number 0-911521-29-1
Printed in the United States of America

Cover design by Teresa Tam
Production: Grace Light, Teresa Tam

PHOTO CREDITS

Cover . . . . 1984 Dogwood Relays 100m, by Bill Killian
11. . . . . .Ade Mafe (GB), by Stewart Kendall
14. . . . . Lyudmila Kondratyeva, by Horstmüller
21. . . . . Alice Brown, by Victor Sailer/Agence Shot
28. . . . . .Merlene Ottey, by Jon Hardesty
32. .Thomas Schönlebe, by Stewart Kendall
39. . . . . Darren Clark, by Claus Andersen/ALLSPORT
41. . . . . Diane Dixon, by Victor Sailer/Agence Shot
54. . . . . .Valeriy Borzov, by Peter Probst
71. . . . . Chandra Cheeseborough, by Bill Leung, Jr.
73. . . . . Natalya Kovtun, by ALLSPORT/Gray Mortimore
77. . . . . .Irena Szewinska, by DUOMO/Gale Constable
80. . . . . .Florence Griffith Joyner, by Mike Voudoris/Sailer Ltd.
97. .Allan Wells, by ALLSPORT/Tony Duffy
104. . . . . Pietro Mennea, by Mark Shearman
112. . . . . .Grit Breuer, by Claus Andersen/ALLSPORT
113. . . . . .1983 Texas Relays 4 x 400, by Charles Parker
120. . . . . .1984 NCAA Championships 4 x 100, by Kevin Morris

ACKNOWLEDGEMENTS

The publishers wish to thank the following publications for their cooperation and permission to reprint articles that originally appeared in their pages:

ATHLETICS COACH, Julie Dennis, Editor. Published by the British Amateur Athletic Board, Edgbaston House, 3 Duchess Place, Hagley Road, Birmingham B16 8NM, England.

DER LEICHTATHLET, Peter Gran, Editor. Published by Deutscher Verband fur Leichtathletik der DDR, Dimitroffstrasse 157, Berlin 1055, German Democratic Republic.

DIE LEHRE DER LEICHTATHLETIK, published as part of *Leichtathletik.* Helmar Hommel, Editor.

EUROPEAN ATHLETIC COACHES XVth CONGRESS REPORT, Bad Blankenburg, German Democratic Republic, 1989.

ERUNDLAGEN DER LEICHTATHLETIK, Karl-Heinz Bauersfeld and Gerd Schroter, Editors. Published by Sportverlag Berlin, Neustadtische Kirchstrasse 15 , Berlin 1086, German Democratic Republic.

KENAKULTUUR, Ronald Hurt, Editor. Published by Perioodika, Tallinn 200 102, Suur-Karja 11, Estonia, USSR.

KIIRJOOKS, By Hans Torim. Published by Vilde Pedagogical Instituut, Tallinn, Estonia, USSR.

LEICHTATHLETIK, Heinz Vogel, Editor. Published by Dentscher Sportverlag Kurt Stroof GMBH & Co., Eintrachtstrasse 110-118, 5000 Kohn 1, Federal Republic of Germany.

LEGKAYA ATLETIKA, 103021 Moscow K-31, Rodjeatvensk Bulvar 10/7, USSR.

MODERN ATHLETE AND COACH, Jess Jarver, Editor. Published by Australian Track and Field Coaches Association, 1 Fox Avenue, Athlestone, S.A. 5076, Australia.

SPORDILEHT, Mati Eliste, Editor. Rataskaevu 2, Tallinn 200101, Estonia, USSR.

SPORTSWOMAN TOWARDS 2000 CONFERENCE REPORT, Adelaide, S.A., Australia 1988.

TEORIA I PRAKTIKA FIZISHKOI KULTURY, published in Moscow, USSR.

TRACK & FIELD JOURNAL, Roger Burrows, Editor. Published by the Canadian Track and Field Association, 1600 James Naismith Drive, Gloucester, Ontario, K1B 5N4, Canada.

TRACK & FIELD QUARTERLY REVIEW, George G. Dales, Editor. Published by the NCAA Division 1 Track Coaches Association, 1705 Evanston, Kalamazoo, Michigan 49008, USA.

TRACK TECHNIQUE, Jed Goldfried, Editor. Published by Track & Field News, 2570 El Camino Real, No. 606, Mountain View, California 94040, USA.

TABLE OF CONTENTS

CHAPTER III: THE FEMALE SPRINTER

CHAPTER IV: TALENT DEVELOPMENT

CHAPTER V: SPRINT RELAYS

INTRODUCTION

CONTEMPORARY DEVELOPMENTS IN SPRINTING

by Jess Jarver

Looking through the latest information published around the world on the development of sprinting technique and training methods to improve sprinting speed shows that we are still faced with some confusing and contradictory aspects. As some of these aspects appear in this text, please keep in mind that the selection of the articles has purposefully avoided one-sided views. The different opinions, representing the views by authors from many countries, are therefore meant to draw the readers' attention to the fact that many aspects in sprinting are still debatable.

However one looks at it, there is little doubt that sprint performances, depending largely on hereditary characteristics of muscle fiber distribution and neuromuscular coordination, have improved at a slow rate in comparison to most other track and field events. An exception to this was the amazing breakthrough by Florence Griffith Joyner, whose world records cleared the way to new discussions and analysis of sprint techniques and training methods.

Griffith Joyner's enormous improvement once again drew attention to the often analyzed aspects of the stride length, the stride frequency and the velocity curves. Some of these are included in this text by Levtshenko of the USSR and Frank Dick of Great Britain, both presenting some new and interesting views.

Both authors agree that Griffith Joyner's improvement was due to significantly improved strength and power levels, as well as the ability to maintain near maximal velocity for longer than any other athlete. Dick came to the conclusion that there could perhaps be two different approaches to the 100m sprint. One approach is to attain maximal velocity as soon as possible and therefore rely on better speed endurance and speed

maintenance qualities, the second is to utilize a delayed acceleration phase to achieve maximal velocity at a later stage, as demonstrated by Griffith Joyner.

As far as the development of sprinting speed is concerned, it is generally accepted that it depends on an optimal combination of stride length and stride frequency. However, it should be noted that opinions differ on what can be described as an optimal combination. Dr. Winfried Joch of West Germany sums it up by stating that stride frequency and stride length are in sprinting closely related, but it is generally not clear under which conditions does the stride frequency or the stride length become the primary performance deciding component.

Dr. Joch's analysis of the top sprinters in Seoul showed that there is no rule for the time when the longest strides and the highest stride frequency occurs. Johnson and Drechsler, for example, took almost the identical number of strides, were close in maximal and minimal stride length, but differ in stride frequency in favor to Johnson. Griffith Joyner had an average stride length of 2.40m, between 60 and 90m, the same as Drechsler. However, she had an average stride frequency of 4.58 per second in contrast to Drechsler's 4.37 per second.

Levtshenko of the USSR, on the other hand, suggests that coaches should exploit the athlete's natural potential by either increasing stride length and stride frequency, or by reducing one component and increasing noticeably the other component. The optimal approach will then be based on a model that is determined by the athlete's leg length and a module stride coefficient.

Different views are also common on the training procedures in sprinting. Valeriy Borzov, discussing the subject, appears to be convinced that all performance factors have to be developed in an optimal relationship to each other, because an overdevelopment of one factor can frequently be responsible for a drop in another performance area. For example, an improvement in speed endurance can take place at the cost of a drop in pure speed.

This leads to the question of whether sprinting training should be versatile, or should sprinters specialize in one particular distance. Specialists from the Soviet Union fail to agree. Tabatshnik, for example, recommends specialization, claiming that speed endurance in the 100m depends largely on the capacity of the organism to exploit anaerobic-alactic energy, while speed endurance in the 200m is closely related to the anaerobic-lactic system. Different training means are therefore needed for each distance.

Maslakova, in contrast, recommends a versatile approach for female sprinters, while Ozolin suggests a compromise where versatile preparations form the base for specialization in sprint training and lead to outstanding performances.

It is interesting to note here that Canadian national hurdles coach, Brent McFarlane, considers questionable that speed training affects the energy system involved, namely anaerobic-alactic. However, he agrees that the basic sequencing of loads and correct overloading methods on the body seem to have a very positive influence on speed development.

It appears that authorities all over the world are generally agreeable that strength and power development play a very important part in sprint training. Bounding, depth jumping and jumping exercises are recommended by all, particularly when the power development methods allow for an optimal inter and intramuscular coordination that turn the maximal strength potential into high quality dynamic movements.

The random selection of articles in this text, as well as a number of papers presented at the 1989 European Coaches' Association Conference in Bad Blankenberg, German Democratic Republic, reinforce the need to understand the importance of strength and power training in sprinting. Many believe that the success of Griffith Joyner was the direct result of improved stride length, in other words, improved sprinting strength.

When it comes to new developments it is impossible not to draw attention to the sprinting power study by Lemaire and Robertson of Canada that produced a number of new insights into the mechanics of sprinting. The results of their power analysis indicated that the hip muscles are the main movers of the leg throughout the swinging phase. This suggests that the hip flexors and extensors should receive more attention in the sprinter's weight training program and the present emphasis on knee extension and leg curl exercises should be reduced.

The authors also claim that "although the relative importance of the various leg segments to the stride are different, it is important to realize that these powers were obtained during a movement of the entire leg, not from an isolated contraction of one joint." This implies that training must involve the entire leg complex and not just a single joint.

In summary it can be said that if you are looking for revolutionary changes in the contemporary approach to sprint training or technique in this text, you will be disappointed. There have been no drastic changes, although some developments and trends have occurred, due mainly to a more practical help and cooperation of sport scientists.

It also appears that more attention has been paid lately to several aspects that previously were looked at as being of secondary importance. Among these are the importance of strength development, improved restoration methods and a better understanding of stride length and stride frequency in the different phases of sprint races.

At the same time, opinions on several aspects in sprinting still differ slightly on the ways and means to develop sprint talent, improve speed and find the most efficient running technique. This, no doubt, will become obvious to the reader right in the first chapter, dealing with the modern concepts in sprinting. As no attempt has been made in the selection of the material to provide uniformity, it will be up to the coach or athlete to sort out what is best suited and applicable in each individual situation.

CHAPTER I:
MODERN CONCEPTS

SPRINTING—VERSATILITY OR SPECIALIZATION?

by B. Tabatshnik, L. Maslakova, E. Ozolin, USSR

Should sprint training be versatile, or should sprinters specialize in one particular distance? The subject is discussed by three Soviet authors—Tabatshnik, recommending specialization for male sprinters, Maslakova, suggesting a versatile approach for women and Ozolin, claiming a compromise where a versatile preparation forms base for specialization.

SPECIALIZATION

Some years ago it was agreed that top level sprinters should be capable of producing equally fast times in both short sprints. Is such a versatility really possible?

History shows that only eight athletes have succeeded in scoring the Olympic 100 and 200m double. Only three, Bob Morrow (1956), Valeriy Borzov (1972) and Carl Lewis (1984) have won both Olympic sprints since 1956. The world rankings, since the introduction of electric timing, reveal that seven of the 10 fastest 100m exponents fail to make the leading 25 in the 200m (20.50 sec.). On the other hand, five of the first 10 in the 200m (20.10 sec.), are missing from the best 25 in the 100m (10.15 sec.).

This apparent specialization in one sprint is influenced by the improved times and increasingly tougher competition. It is extremely difficult to compete in such meetings as the World and European Championships, Olympic Games, European Cup, etc., often requiring a large number of full effort starts. There appears to be a need for specialization, although little research is available on the subject. Most studies concentrate on the 100m distance and coaches have been inclined to employ similar training for both events.

Looking at the specificity of the 200m shows that there is a general opinion that a 200m performance is accepted as being very good when it is equal, or deviates only a little, from the double of the 100m time, $T200 = 2 \times T100 \pm 0.4$ (Pokrovsi) applies to hand timing, while Gross of U.S.A. recommends $T200 = 2 \times T100 \pm 0.13$ for electric timing.

Gross, analyzing the results of the 1972 Olympics, indicated that good sprinters were dominating the second half of the 200m distance. Athletes in the 20.00 to 21.16 sec. time range, who were faster over the first 100m, were as a rule stronger over the second 100m. This regularity did not occur in sprinters with 21.26 to 21.89 sec. 200m times and Gross reached the conclusion that only high level sprinters are capable of compensating the lack of sufficient maximum speed by speed endurance.

The difference of times between the first and second half in the 200m is regarded as a reliable indicator in evaluating a sprinter's speed endurance. Taking into consideration that about 1.45 sec. is lost in the first half in the start and approximately 1.25 ± 0.2 sec. in running around the curve, top athletes lose 0.73 sec. in the second half of the distance. Lower level performers, on the other hand, lose 1.12 seconds. These figures stress the need to develop speed endurance, so that the second 100m can be covered with minimal losses of speed.

It is known that 100m performances are decided mainly by the athlete's maximal speed capacity and the rate of acceleration. The 200m results, in turn, depend mainly on speed endurance and the level of maximum speed. Speed endurance in the 100m depends largely on the capacity of the organism to exploit anaerobic-alactic energy, while speed endurance in the 200m is closely related to anaerobic-lactic acid system. Coaches must therefore be aware of the differences in the methods required to develop alactic and glycolysis anaerobic systems.

The different demands of the 100 and 200m sprints explain why not all athletes can perform with equal success over both distances. Their success over one or the other distance depends largely on specializing according to their anthropometric measurements. Athletes who are good in the 100m but weak in the 200m, are usually relatively tall (174.4 cm) and heavy (73.2 kg) with a height-weight index of 1.2. Sprinters, who excel in the 200m, are on an average 182.9 cm tall, weigh 71.8 kg and have an index of 11.1.

Athletes with different morphological indicators achieve maximum speed differently. Tall sprinters have longer strides and lower stride frequency in comparison to medium height runners. They cover the 100m in 44 to 46 strides and perform well in the 200m. Shorter athletes use 48 to 52 strides in the 100m and usually perform well only over short distances.

The maintenance of a high work capacity level depends largely on a rational exploitation of energy reserves. Athletes with longer strides usually use energy rationally and quickly replace used energy reserves. A high stride frequency, on the other hand, is responsible for rapidly accumulating fatigue. This means excellent results in the 100m but restricts 200m performance.

Research information reveals that speed in the 100 and 200m races drops mainly through a reduction in stride frequency. There is normally no change in the stride length, showing that fatigue results from a drop of stride frequency and is responsible for speed losses in the 100m and particularly in the 200m. Further, an analysis of the speed dynamics in the 100m shows two groups of sprinters.

The first group is successful mainly because of their excellent reaction time and extremely fast acceleration. They reach maximum speed at the 35 to 45m mark and have a very high stride frequency (5.30 to 5.55 stride/sec.) but only a medium stride length (210 to 220 cm). The speed in this group drops considerably in the second part of the distance (75 to 80m) and is 10 to 11% below the maximum in the last 10m.

The second group covers the 100m in 45 to 47 strides with a gradual acceleration to reach maximum speed after the 50m mark. Their stride length at maximum speed is 230 to 245 cm and the stride frequency 4.55 to 4.70 stride/sec. The sprinters in this group, usually 180 to 195cm tall, slow down less in the second part of the distance with the last 10m speed 8 to 9% below the maximum.

The individual differences in the speed dynamics are decided by the sensitivity of the athlete's nervous system. Fast accelerating sprinters, who perform well over 60 and 100m, have a weak but very sensitive nervous system. Those with good speed endurance but slower acceleration, who perform well over 200m, usually possess a strong but not so sensitive nervous system.

The above concepts aid in selecting the best distance for a sprinter at the age of 17 to 18 years, provided the young athlete has been training at least three or four years. The evaluation parameters are listed in Table 1.

VERSATILITY

Women sprinters, in contrast to their male counterparts, contest successfully two or three sprint distances. This tendency has become particularly obvious over the last 10 years, as a rapidly increasing number of women sprinters compete in the 400m. Athletes who have the 100m as their main event, often include 400m races to their early season program to check training progress. Sprinters who concentrate on the 200 and 400m distances, include 400m races in the program in the second half of the season, prior to important major meets.

It is interesting to note that high level performances in all three sprint distances have been achieved by women sprinters with the best 200m times. The 200m requires a high level of speed endurance as all parts of the distance have to be covered with a maximum effort. This requires a certain amount of versatility in training and

Table 1: Model indicators for 17 to 18 year old sprinters.

Indicator	100m 10.80 - 11.00 sec.	200m 21.40 - 22.00 sec.
Height (cm)	165-175	175-185
Weight (kg)	65-75	65-75
Crouch start 5m sprint (sec.)	1.30-1.35	1.35-1.40
Crouch start 30m sprint (sec.)	4.15-4.20	4.25-4.30
1st and 2nd half differences, 100m (sec.)	1.10-1.15	1.20-1.30
1st and 2nd half differences, 200m (sec.)	0.00	0.20
100m number of strides	48-52	46-47
100m stride frequency (stride/sec.)	5.10-4.80	4.60-4.40
Best times differences (T100 x 2-T200) sec.	0.60-1.00	0.00±0.20

-B. Tabatshnik

Lyudmila Kondratyeva, USSR, 1980 Olympic 100m Champion

appears to be responsible for improved times in all three sprint distances.

These facts should convince coaches of women sprinters the need to employ a versatile training approach. Unfortunately practical experience reveals that our leading coaches tend to prefer specialization.

—L. Maslakova

COMBINING SPECIALIZATION WITH VERSATILITY

The previous two articles appear to indicate that men and women sprinters take different roads to the top. Men are in the main specializing in one sprint distance, while women are using a versatile approach. These different approaches are reflected also in the world records when the average running speeds in setting the records are compared (see Table 2).

Table 2: Average running speed in records (m/sec.)

Distance	Men		Women	
	World	U.S.S.R.	World	U.S.S.R.
100m	10.07	9.93	9.29	9.19
200m	10.14	10.00	9.21	9.01
400m	9.12	8.96	8.33	8.23

As can be seen, the fastest sprint distance for men is the 200m, for women the 100m. Looking at the dynamics of the running speed shows that men hold close to maximum speed for 150 to 160m when it drops by 6 to 8%. This is responsible for a faster average speed in the 200m. The 200m speed begins to drop around the 130 to 140m mark for women and is reduced by 10 to 12%. A typical example of what happens is shown in a 22.66 sec. race of Olympic 100m champion Kondratyeva (see Table 3).

It should be noted that 9.43 m/sec was not Kondratyeva's maximum speed. She reached in her best 100m races 10.5 m/sec. It underlines the fact that women's 200m records, in comparison to men, are not of a high standard and are likely to be improved in the near future.

Why are women unable to maintain near maximum running speed in the longer sprint? Physiological differences appear to be responsible for this. It is known that women are well behind the men in power capacities but a lot less in endurance factors. Consequently, women sprinters train less in the high intensity zone, running basically longer distances at optimal speeds. Men, on the other hand, employ a lot more sprinting at maximum speeds.

Psychological factors also appear to play a part when it comes to competitions. Male 200m sprinters approach the distance with a maximum acceleration, attempt to reach maximum running speed and try to maintain it as long as possible. Female sprinters employ changing speed patterns, including a free running out of the curve.

Success in the short sprint depends on how effectively an athlete can exploit all running performances components—the start, a fast acceleration, maximum running speed and the maintenance of it to the end of the distance. All this is decided by versatility in training, as top performers can't afford to have a weak link. Borzov and Mennea, who were capable of fast times over several distances, are typical examples.

Contemporary competition, on the other hand, requires narrow specialization. It is therefore important to emphasize starting and acceleration in 100m training, while attention in the 200m training is directed to curve running and the maintenance of maximum speed.

Consequently, it is possible to say, without hesitation, that versatile preparation forms the base for specialization in sprint training and leads to outstanding performances.

—E. Ozolin

Table 3: Kondratyeva's speed in 200m

Distance (m)	110	120	130	140	150	160	170	180	190	200
Speed (m/sec)	9.43	9.43	9.43	9.43	9.25	9.09	8.77	8.94	8.33	8.19

POWER IN SPRINTING

by E.D. Lemaire and D.G.E. Robertson, Canada

A study of the definition and development of power in sprinting that has produced a number of new insights into the mechanics of the pure speed events.

INTRODUCTION AND DEFINITIONS

Power. The word conjures instant images of explosiveness, strength, brute force, and athletic prowess. In fact, in the world of sports there are few words that are used with such regularity and scope ("What a powerful throw", "He's a powerhouse", "C'mon, do it with a bit more power").

It becomes apparent that the term power has been used in many ways but, in the world of biomechanics, power has a much less abstract meaning. Average power is defined as the amount of mechanical work done in a specific period of time or in equational terms:

$$P = \frac{W}{t} \quad \text{where } \begin{aligned} P &= \text{power} \\ W &= \text{mechanical work} \\ t &= \text{time} \end{aligned}$$

In the above equation, the term "work" refers to the amount of energy required to raise the body against gravity or to increase the speed of the body. Power, therefore, is the measure of the ability to do the most work in the least amount of time. In the world of athletics there is no event that requires more power than sprinting (measured in the same units as electrical power, watts (W)).

Average power, while being a useful measure for simple tasks (such as lifting or jumping), is not appropriate for locomotor tasks. For example, the average power produced by an 80.0Kg sprinter who finishes the 100m dash at a speed of 12 m/s would be approximately 576 watts (5760 joules of work done). This value represents a fraction of the peak power required for this same sprinter to flex one leg while running at the speed of 12 m/s. Instantaneous power is of more use in the analysis of human performance since the power required to drive the various parts of the body can be attributed to specific muscle groups. The only limitation, unfortunately, is that it is not mathematically possible to attribute the exact amounts of force and power to a particular muscle within these groups. The equation for instantaneous power is:

$$P = Mw \quad \text{where } \begin{aligned} P &= \text{power} \\ M &= \text{moment} \\ &\quad \text{(turning effect)} \\ &\quad \text{of a force} \\ w &= \text{angular velocity} \end{aligned}$$

In a human body, muscles exert their forces against the levers of the body, the bones. These forces are exerted obliquely to the long axes of the bones and, therefore cause turning effects which, in biomechanics, are called moments of force. The greater the force, the greater the moment of force. Also, the more perpendicular the force to the long axis of the bone the greater will be its turning effect. The standard unit for moments of force is the newton met (N.m.)

Angular velocity is the term given to the speed of rotation of an object. This is usually measured in radians per second or degrees per second. One radian per second is equivalent to approximately 57 degrees per second. One revolution per second is equivalent to approximately 6.3 (2 pi) radians per second.

In the 100m sprint, work must be done to rotate the body's segments, to restore the energy lost during landing, and to propel the body forward. When sprinting at high speeds this work must be done in a short amount of time. For top sprinters a full stride takes approximately 0.45 seconds. It becomes obvious that the ability to perform work in a short time span is a critical factor to sprinting.

Muscles can produce concentric and eccentric

Table 1: Work and peak powers of the knee and hip moments of force for sprinters.

Table 1(a) SPRINT POWER MEN (OUTDOOR 50-55m)

| | HIP | | | | | | KNEE | | | | | |
| | Flexor Concentric | | Extensor Eccentric | | Extensor Concentric | | Extensor Eccentric | | Extensor Concentric | | Flexor Eccentric | |
Subject	Work	Power	Work	Power	Work	Power	Work	Power	Work	Power	Work	Power
1	239	4124	-14	-406	288	3243	-204	-2908	4	196	-287	-4872
2	259	3308	-12	-382	239	3163	-190	-2539	5	158	-284	-4592
3	156	2475	-7	-324	164	1684	-95	-1578	21	636	-159	-2730
Average	218	3302	-11	-371	230	2696	-163	-2342	10	330	-243	-4064
S. Dev.	45	825	3	35	51	717	49	561	8	217	60	951

Table 1(b) SPRINT POWER MEN (INDOOR 30-35m)

| | HIP | | | | | | KNEE | | | | | |
| | Flexor Concentric | | Extensor Eccentric | | Extensor Concentric | | Extensor Eccentric | | Extensor Concentric | | Flexor Eccentric | |
Subject	Work	Power	Work	Power	Work	Power	Work	Power	Work	Power	Work	Power
1	149	1794	-2	-100	183	2016	-96	-1196	5	141	-175	-2155
2	133	1471	-9	-232			-82	-907	1	96		
3	167	1262	-3	-73	66	946	-76	-1003	1	51	-98	-1358
4	155	1591	-15	-409	190	2086	-120	-1326			-190	-2696
5			-41	-745	117	1322			0	5	-81	-893
6	197	2286	-10	-334	223	2348	-125	-1581	4	138	-204	-2546
Average	160	1638	-13	-316	156	1744	-100	-1203	2	86	-150	-1930
S. Dev.	21	348	13	225	56	523	19	284	1	52	50	695

Table 1(c) SPRINT POWER WOMEN (OUTDOOR 50-55m)

| | HIP | | | | | | KNEE | | | | | |
| | Flexor Concentric | | Extensor Eccentric | | Extensor Concentric | | Extensor Eccentric | | Extensor Concentric | | Flexor Eccentric | |
Subject	Work	Power	Work	Power	Work	Power	Work	Power	Work	Power	Work	Power
1	112	1086	-5	-164	147	1936	-113	-1166	1	49	-153	-2243
2	170	2074	-15	-473	171	1708	-90	-1100	0	38	-169	-2501
3	131	1729	-7	-278	189	2553	-85	-849	10	354	-191	-2605
4	106	1122	-11	-334	98	1084	-79	-995	3	125	-117	-2049
5	117	1391	-2	-96	128	1373	-106	-1303	4	200	-171	-2615
Average	127	1480	-8	-269	147	1731	-95	-1083	4	153	-161	-2403
S. Dev.	22	670	4	131	32	503	12	153	3	116	24	222

Table 1(d) SPRINT POWER WOMEN (INDOOR 30-35m)

| | HIP | | | | | | KNEE | | | | | |
| | Flexor Concentric | | Extensor Eccentric | | Extensor Concentric | | Extensor Eccentric | | Extensor Concentric | | Flexor Eccentric | |
Subject	Work	Power	Work	Power	Work	Power	Work	Power	Work	Power	Work	Power
1	83	622	-7	-216	97	1145	-67	-742	3	94	-113	-1597
2	92	1108	-1	-51	99	839	-65	-750	1	37	-101	-1548
3	108	1023	-2	-73	132	1227	-76	-905 A	1	41	-153	-2222
4	94	943	-6	-194	104	1419	-87	-1030	0	23	-133	-1896
5	133	1165	-5	-144	131	1499	-82	-1034	8	210	-161	-2358
6	103	1058	-1	-57	63	708	-75	-794	1	57	-110	-1721
7	94	887	-1	-61	96	985	-77	-995	2	65	-116	-1748
Average	102	987	-4	-122	104	1140	-75	-876	2	77	-128	-1890
S. Dev.	15	177	2	66	23	286	7	122	2	63	22	305

work. Concentric work involves a muscle shortening while contracting (i.e., the muscle acts to create motion at a joint). Eccentric work, on the other hand, involves the muscle lengthening while contracting (i.e., the muscle acts to oppose the motion at a joint, seeking to slow down or stop that motion). The importance of concentric work is generally understood (since without it there would be no motion) but eccentric work is also very important in injury prevention, shock absorption, control of the rate of motion, storage of elastic energy, and stopping of the limbs.

To identify movements of body parts and the moments of force that are acting to cause or inhibit movements a special naming system is used. Figure 1 shows the terms used to define the names of the directions of motion of the three joints of the leg.

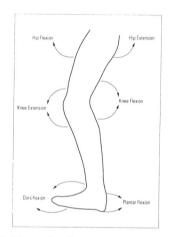

Figure 1: Name for the directions of motion of the three leg joints.

METHODS AND RESULTS

To examine the powers produced in sprinting, races of 50m (indoors) and 100m (outdoors) were analyzed. In both cases the races were conducted under very competitive conditions (indoor world records for men's and women's 50m were set at the indoor meet) and involved internationally ranked Canadian and American sprinters. A total of 8 sprint races were filmed using a high speed camera set at 100 frames per second for the outdoor races and 50 frames per second for the indoor races (because of insufficient lighting). These films were digitized using a semiautomated computer system which was capable of computing the speeds, accelerations, moments of force, energies, and powers at the hip, knee, and ankle joints. The outdoor sprints were filmed from 50 to 55 meters while the indoor sprints were filmed from 30 to 35 meters. Once the data were collected and processed

the resultant information was tabulated and compared on the basis of powers produced by the muscles crossing the leg joints during the swing phase. Figure 2 shows a stick figure representing the swing leg used in the analysis. The figure represents the trunk, thigh, shank and foot segments from the left side of the body.

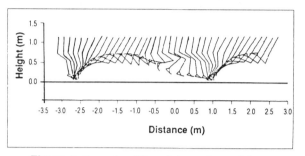

Figure 2: Sample of the data collected from one sprint stride.

The analysis of the sprint stride is summarized in Table 1. The table is divided into four parts corresponding to the indoor and outdoor races for males and females. These four tables are subdivided into the peak work and the peak power values for each burst of power produced at the hip and knee joints.

HIP POWER

The first burst of power from the hip muscles during the swing-through was produced by the hip flexors (muscles that cross the front of the hip, such as the ilio-psoas and rectus femoris) acting to drive the thigh and knee upwards and forwards. These power values were the largest incurred during the sprint stride with the top male athletes reaching approximately 4100 W (enough power turn on forty-one 100 watt light bulbs) and the top female reaching 2100 W during the outdoor races. The second power burst at the hip was produced by the hip extensors (gluteal muscles) performing negative work (i.e., the hip extensor muscles acted eccentrically to slow down the rising leg). Power values for this burst were the smallest of the three hip power bursts (maxima: for males = -750 w, for females = -470 W). The final hip power burst was produced again by the hip extensors performing positive work to drive the leg to the ground. Maximal power values were 3200 W for men and 2500 W for women. Curiously, the women consistently had larger bursts of extensor power than flexor power while the men produced larger flexor powers. This may indicate a weakness in the ability of the female athletes in producing hip flexor power.

KNEE POWER

Power values for the knee were much different from the hip. From Figure 4 it can be seen that the first power burst from the knee was produced by eccentric contraction by the knee extensors (since the power was negative). The maximum power values for this phase were -1300 W for females and -2500 for males. The second phase for the knee involved low positive powers (200 W for males and 140 W for females) produced by a concentric action of the extensors. The final power contribution to the knee motion was eccentric in nature and produced by the flexors (i.e., the hamstring muscle group working to slow down knee extension). The maximum powers for this phase were -4800 W for the men and -2300 for the women. The maximal knee concentric power values, as compared to the hip, are observed to be 15-20 times smaller. It is only eccentrically that the knee produces substantial power (6-12 times greater than maximum hip eccentric power).

INDOOR vs. OUTDOOR

Another trend that appeared was that the work and power results of the indoor trials were much less than the results for the outdoor trials. This is accounted for by the fact that the indoor racers had not reached their top speeds at 30m from the start.

To compare among the subjects, the means and standard deviations of each section were calculated and displayed under the appropriate column. Missing values in the tables are due to differences in stride length and frequency of the runners which prevented the capture of a complete stride for some runners. The number of subjects in each area also varied due to the difficulties in isolating specific runners in a close race (in all cases the fastest runners were analyzed).

Although the numbers associated with the peak work and peak powers are necessary when comparing individuals, it is useful to have a graphical display of the patterns of power produced. Angular velocities, joint movements, and joint powers for the hip and knee of a male sprinter are displayed in Figures 3 and 4, respectively.

To relate these graphs to the actual motion, vertical lines representing specific events in the running stride were placed on the graph. The ITO (ipsolateral toe-off) line represents the point where the toe of the measured leg leaves the ground; CFS (contralateral foot strike) represents first contact of the opposite foot on the ground; CTO represents the contralateral foot leaving the ground; and IFS

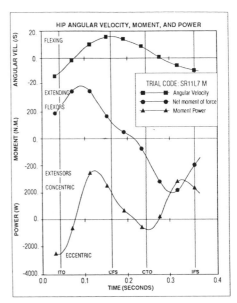

Figure 3: Angular velocity, moment of force, and power produced at the hip by a male sprinter at the midway point of a 100m dash.

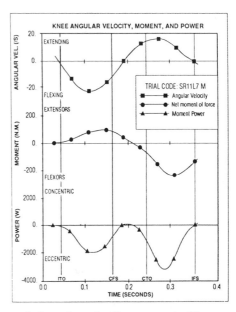

Figure 4: Angular velocity, moment of force, and power produced at the knee by a male sprinter at the midway point of a 100m dash.

represents the return of the measured leg to the ground.

The top curve of each graph is an angular velocity of the joint in question. From the angular velocity tracing, the maximum velocity for hip extension was approximately 16 rad/s (912 deg/s) and was 17 rad/s (969 deg/s) for hip flexion. The knee angular velocities (extension = 21 rad/s, 1200 deg/s); flexion = 18 rad/s, 1030 rad/s) were larger than the hip angular velocities. The angular velocity curve is also helpful in locating the exact time when the joint changes from flexion to extension. The second curve displays the moments about the joint. This curve is used to determine when the flexor or extensor muscles are dominant in the motion at any point in time. The bottom curve is the instantaneous power produced by the moment of force of the muscle at the joint plotted against time. From here the concentric or eccentric component of the motion can be determined. A positive power value indicates concentric work while a negative value for instantaneous power represents eccentric work. It is also possible to read the peak powers from this plot, locate the positions of the peak powers and examine the trends in joint power production.

In addition to the power analyses, the speed of several athletes over the last portion of their 100m outdoor race was also measured. From Figure 5 it was found that the top male sprinter was able to reach a speed of 12 m/s (43Km/h) after the first 60 meters and maintain that speed for the remainder of the race. The top female sprinter reached a top speed of 10 m/s (36Km/h) and was also able to maintain this speed to the finish.

DISCUSSION
HIP, KNEE, ANKLE: THE DIFFERENCE

The hip exhibited substantial concentric power output for both flexion and extension with relatively two eccentric power values. This result indicates an active role by the hip in driving the leg through and back during a sprint stride. The knee muscles, on the other hand, acted primarily as shock absorbers over the same time period with high eccentric powers in the extension and flexion phases and a relatively low concentric extension power during mid-swing. These results support the view that the knee muscles make essentially no contribution to the speed or height of the leg in the swing phase. Thus, the hip muscles are responsible for most of the leg's motion while the knee muscles act mainly to slow the motion at the knee (this slowing down at the knee is essential so as to prevent hyper-extension and hyperstretch problems). It follows that muscular training of the hip flexors and extensors should receive a much higher priority in an athlete's training than the muscular training of the knee flexors and extensors.

INDOOR vs. OUTDOOR

The data from this study show substantial differences in the powers produced between the indoor trials and the outdoor trials. These differences can be accounted for by the higher

sprinting speeds attained during the outdoor trials. This speed discrepancy can be accounted for by the different areas over which the data was collected (the outdoor trials were filmed from 30 to 35 meters and the indoor trials were filmed from 50 to 66 meters).

Figure 5 shows that during the outdoor trials peak speed was not reached until 60 meters or after.

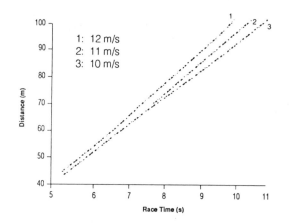

Figure 5: Positions and average speeds of three sprinters over the final portion of an outdoor 100m dash (1=male, t=10.06 s; 2=male, t=10.53 s; 3=female, t=10.53 s).

MALE vs. FEMALE

Comparison of the results obtained by the males and females were not surprising. The male athletes achieved powers that were approximately 100% greater than the female athletes. This difference can be attributed to the larger weight of the males (more work must be done to move a larger weight), and their greater running speed. It should be noted, though, that the men and women both had the same patterns of power generation and absorption.

CONCLUSION

This study of sprinters has produced a number of new insights into the mechanics of sprinting. For example, although it has long been felt that sprinters decelerate at the end of a race it is now apparent that very well trained sprinters can maintain their maximum speed until the end of a 100m sprint. It is also apparent that these same sprinters have a maximum velocity that is reached somewhere between 60 and 70 meters.

Although many coaches put great emphasis on knee extension and leg curl exercises in their sprint training programs, the results of these power

1984 Olympic 100m silver medalist Alice Brown, the picture of power and explosiveness

analyses would indicate that the hip muscles are the main movers of the leg throughout the whole swing phase. This would suggest to the coach that the hip flexors and extensors should receive more attention in a sprinter's weight training program than would the knee musculature. The knee flexors, however, do perform eccentrically at relatively high levels for both flexion and extension; therefore, they should be trained for this type of work. Exercises such as depth jumping, bounding, and decline running should provide the correct training stimulus.

Although the relative importance of the various leg segments to the stride are different, it is important to realize that these powers were obtained during a movement of the entire leg, not from an isolated contraction of one joint. This implies that training must also be done with the entire leg complex, not just a single joint. Without the balanced coordination of all power producing muscles maximal leg speed and power may not be achievable.

ACKNOWLEDGEMENTS

This research was conducted with the help and the support of Mr. Gerard Mach, Ms. Maria Mach, and Mr. Pat Reid. The authors would like to thank Mr. Jean-Marie Wilson, Mr. Daniel Curry, and Mr. Donald Bradley for their technical assistance. Financial support for this research was provided by the Sport Science Support Program of Sport Canada.

DIMENSIONS OF MOTOR SPEED

by Professor Dr. Winfried Joch, West Germany

An overview of the recent information on speed performance factors, including reaction speed, acceleration, stride frequency and stride length in sprinting.

Speed is an essential component in a sporting performance. Speed belongs with strength, endurance and mobility to the "motor qualities", or "basic qualities", or "motor capacities". In track and field it is normally measured as the time interval required to cover a certain distance—100m (= distance) in 11.0 seconds (time interval). Next to the usual sporting concept of speed, there is the concept of velocity. Velocity (v) is defined as the relationship between the covered distance (s) and the time (t) required for it. The formula is:

$$v = \frac{s \text{ (measured in meters)}}{t \text{ (measured in seconds)}}$$

or: meters per second.

For example, Ben Johnson in the Seoul Olympic final reached his highest velocity, 12.04m/sec. between 50 and 60m, finishing in 9.79 seconds. Carl Lewis ran 9.92 seconds, 0.13 seconds slower, yet his maximal velocity (m/sec.) also achieved between 50 and 60m, and was equal to Johnson's.

Velocity applies to both cyclic and acyclic movements. Cyclic movements are denoted as movements with repetitive part-phases, such as walking, running, swimming and rowing. Acyclic movements are such movement patterns where part-phases are not repeated, such as throwing and jumping.

1. REACTIONS

Three different stimulants, responsible for different reaction times, can be distinguished in the reaction speed. The human reacts the fastest to a touching stimulus. The time is given as 0.10-0.18 seconds. The reaction time to acoustic signals ranges between 0.12-0.18 seconds and to optical signals between 0.15-0.18 seconds.

It should be taken into consideration that these figures differ considerably according to the measuring methods of the reaction time or the apparatus (reaction meter). This physiological law is used to set 0.10 seconds as the lowest level of the reaction performance and times below 0.10 seconds are considered as "anticipated".

The different reaction performances—touch, acoustic and optic—are specific. This means that the one who reacts very fast to an optical signal, can react slower to an acoustic signal and vice versa. This, for example, is important in relays, where the first runner, as in sprint races, reacts to an acoustic signal, all others however to a visual signal.

There is a basic difference between simple reactions and choice reactions. Simple reactions are based on the performance of a previously defined movement (in sprinting the starting action) following a known signal (the starter's gun). A choice reaction (in the simplest format), for example, takes place in the reaction to an optical signal when a green button has to be pushed when

Table 1: Speed and velocity values of Johnson and Lewis in the 1988 Olympic final in 10m intervals.

B.J.	5.48	9.61	10.75	11.62	11.90	12.04	11.90	11.76	11.49	11.11
	1.83	2.87	3.80	4.66	5.50	6.33	7.17	8.02	8.89	9.79
C.L.	5.29	9.34	10.63	11.23	11.62	12.04	11.76	11.76	11.62	11.38
	1.89	2.96	3.90	4.79	5.65	6.48	7.33	8.18	9.04	9.92

Figure 1: Organization of speed dimensions

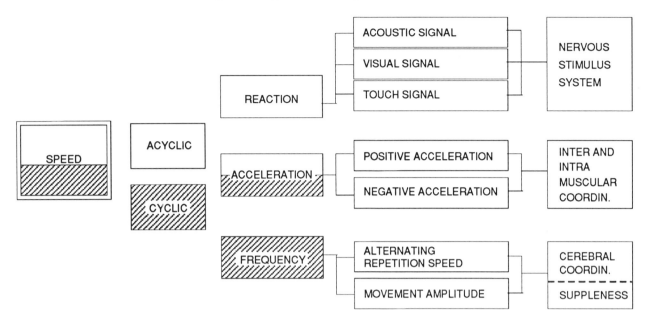

Speed can be broken down into three relatively independent areas or dimensions: reaction, acceleration, frequency.

a green light appears and a red button on the red signal.

According to Zaciorskij there are fine stages in the reaction processes from the signal to the first muscular activity. However, it is sufficient in sporting activities to define reaction time as the time taken from the signal to the first muscular action (reaction time including the latent time).

It is presumed that the reaction time, at least in the sprint start, can be improved through the pre-tension of the muscles (pressure on the blocks in the "set" position), as well as the previously warmed up musculature. This is even more probable when the number of muscles participating in the reaction performances increases.

The question of the trainability of the reaction speed is still a disputed subject. Simkin claims 10 to 20% improvement through training. As a rule there is also a difference between athletes and non-athletes in favor of the athletes. However, this could be the result of conditioning.

Borzov registered at the Munich Olympic Games (1972) in three races a reaction speed of 0.12 seconds. The average for the short sprinters was between 0.16-0.18 seconds. The result of Borzov's indicates that training leads "first of all to a distinct confinement of average variations". There are in normal situations considerable fluctuations in multiple measurements of the reaction.

Information on the reaction times in the 100m start in Seoul 1988 (final) for men and women are shown in Table 2. Particularly noticeable from the information is that Joyner in 13.1 had a faster reaction time than Johnson in 13.2. On the other hand, there was no linear relationship between the reaction times and the 100m times of the athlete.

Table 2: Reaction times in the 100m start in Seoul 1988 (final), measured in 1/100 sec.

Johnson	13.2	Joyner	13.1
Lewis	13.6	Ashford	17.6
Christie	13.8	Drechsler	14.3
Smith	17.6	Jackson	16.8
Mitchell	18.6	Torrence	14.8
Silva	15.5	Pomochnikova	14.1
Williams	14.9	Cuthbert	16.5
Stewart	15.9	Vetchernikova	14.0

The deciding factor in the reaction performance is the functional capacity of the central nervous system (CNS) or, to be more precise, the participation of the sensors system, located in the skin, the muscles, tendons and ligaments for the touching stimulus. The audio system reacts to acoustic and the optical sytem to visual signals. These part-systems are extremely specialized, transmitting through different paths the stimuli to the central nervous sytem. This explains the specificity of the reaction times.

As far as age is concerned, the largest improvements in the reaction time occur between the ages of 7 and 8 for boys and 9 and 10 for girls. Vilkner and Winter denote the first to fourth year in school, or the age of 6/7 to 11/12, as the most favorable age for the improvement of the reaction time. However, the best values were registered at the age of 12. Fomin/Filin, in contrast, claim that "the latent time of the movement reaction of the hand, the movement of the upper arm, the upper and lower leg and the foot is at the age of 13 to 14 years already close to that of adults.

2. ACCELERATION

Acceleration is a measurement of velocity changes in movements. It is defined as the quotient of the velocity changes (∇v) and the time required for it (Λt):

$$\alpha = \frac{\Delta v}{\Lambda t}$$

The measuring unit is meter per second. A positive acceleration takes place when speed over the covered distance is increased, a negative acceleration occurs when the speed over the covered distance is reduced.

A positive acceleration in the 100m sprint, admittedly, takes place only over the first few meters before it is changed to a negative acceleration after maximal velocity has been reached. This point for world's best sprinters is around the 50m mark. As can be seen from Table 1, Johnson and Lewis reach maximal velocity between 50 and 60m, which means that they have accelerated up to this point. Even more impressive are the corresponding values for Joyner (Table 3).

Joyner accelerates to reach her maximal velocity of 10.98 m/sec. between 60 and 70m and maintains this maximal value until 90m. The average acceleration over the section between 70 and 90m is therefore 0. Based on ther above formula, the acceleration is up to 20m positive and after that up to 60m negative: 2.50 - 3.82 - 0.83 - 0.54 - 0.24 - 0.12 - 0.13 .

Newton's second law—strength = mass x acceleration indicates that there is a correlation between strength and acceleration. The available strength is on one hand regulated by the cross section of the muscles, on the other hand by the

inter- and intramuscular coordination. The inter-muscular coordination is responsible for an optimal timing of the action of the muscle groups involved in the planned movement. The intramuscular coordination is responsible for the simultaneous activation of the highest possible number of motor units with the aim to create contraction in all available muscle fibers. The term coordination means here an improvement of the nerve-muscle cohesion. How the available strength can be most efficiently exploited is still a controversial subject of the sprinting technique.

Particularly significant from a biomechanical viewpoint are, above all, "the principle of the optimal acceleration path", as well as "the principle of the beginning strength". The principle of the optimal acceleration path can be summed up as follows: "The available level of muscular strength and coordination capacity has to be used for an optimally long acceleration for body movements that have to reach a high final velocity". The length of an optimally useful acceleration path depends on the proportion of the breaking thrust with the acceleration drive. The principle of the beginning strength reads: "A body movement that has to reach a high final velocity must be initiated by a movement in the opposite direction. The breaking of the opposite movement provides in the beginning a positive strength for acceleration, provided that the transfer occurs fluently. This increases the acceleration drive".

The training of the acceleration capacity, because of the close correlation between acceleration and an optimal strength insertion, is particularly important as far as age is concerned. The close affinity between acceleration and dynamic strength means that each age range, in which particular strength development spurts occur, provides advantages for the improvement of the acceleration capacity. As far as sprinting speed is concerned this means that performances of the complex running speed improves during and after puberty mainly from an increased running stride, because of an optimal correlation between the strength development and the running speed in the 13 to 17 year age range.

The importance of the improvement of the acceleration capacity becomes further evident in the fact that the development of the running speed in the 8 to 15 years age range takes place mainly in the first 4 to 5 seconds of the performance.

Table 3: Time and velocity values of Joyner in 10m intervals.

F.J.	2.00	3.09	4.09	5.04	5.97	6.89	7.80	9.62	10.54
	5.09	9.17	10.00	10.52	10.75	10.86	10.98	10.90	10.86

3. FREQUENCY

The factor of "frequency" in speed is defined as the alternating repetition speed and takes place only in cyclic speed movements. It should be treated from three view points:

- from the viewpoint of the muscle coordination guided by the brain;
- from the viewpoint of the dependence on movement amplitude (stride length in sprinting);
- from the viewpoint of the movement range of the joints (mobility).

Explanations: **1. Muscle coordination:** The movement frequency, as the base for forward propulsion (wings of a bird), depends in principle on the alternating activation of antagonistic muscles. This complicated coordination procedure is guided from the brain. "The cerebral pacemaker is located in the stem of the brain". It must be noted here that a cyclic movement pattern is not simply a chain of reflections.

2. Movement amplitude: It is plausible that speed in a cyclic movement performance depends, next to the cerebral guidance, also on the movement amplitude. This means in sprinting that the stride frequency and the stride length are closely related, although it is generally not clear under which conditions does the stride frequency or the stride length become the primary performance deciding component.

3. Mobility: It is certain that mobility, defined as the movement range of the joints, influences performance. Mobility depends on the elasticity of the muscles, as well as the mechanical construction of the joints and the flexibility of the tendons and ligaments.

In this context it is interesting to note some data on the world's best sprinters in Seoul 1988:

Stride frequency (maximum): Johnson—5.02, Lewis—5.84, Joyner—4.68, Ashford—4.93 (strides per second between 30 and 60m).

Stride frequency (minimum): Johnson—4.61, Lewis—4.15, Joyner—4.35, Drechsler—4.08 (strides per second between 0 and 30m).

Stride length (maximum): Johnson—2.42m, Lewis—2.65m, Joyner—2.40m, Ashford—2.19m, Drechsler—2.40m (between 60 and 90m).

Stride length (minimum): Johnson—1.71m, Lewis—1.85m, Joyner—1.69m, Ashford—1.61m, Drechsler—1.78m (between 0 and 30m).

Total number of strides (0 to 100m): Johnson—46.6, Drechsler—46.4, Lewis—43.6, Ashford—50.8.

Although this is not the place to interpret this data in detail, three remarks nevertheless appear to be in order:

1. There is no rule for the time when the longest strides (largest amplitude) and the highest stride frequency occurs (60 to 90m and 0 to 30m).

2. Johnson and Drechsler take almost the identical number of strides, are close in the maximal and minimal stride length, but differ in the stride frequency in favor to Johnson. Their time difference exceeds one second.

3. Joyner has between 60 and 90m an averge stride length of 2.40m, the same as Drechsler. However, she has an average stride frequency of 4.58, in contrast to Drechsler's 4.37 per second.

There is a relatively close agreement among the authors in regard to the stride frequency as far as age is concerned. All stress that it is largely dependent on the development of the central nervous system and one of the speed capacities that can be developed early at the pre-puberty age.

The conditions for high frequency movements appear to be most favorable between the ages of 8 and 10 years. The conditions and the rate of improvement are the best in this age range. The stride frequency in the tenth year of age reaches 4.4 strides per second for boys and 4.0 strides per second for the girls (average values of untrained persons). There is hardly any difference in the stride frequency at this age between the youngsters and the best sprinters.

The capacity to maintain a constant movement frequency is recorded as being the best for 7- to 8-year-old girls and 13- to 14-year-old boys. According to Israel, children reach their final running stride frequency already at the age of 8 years (similar to pianists and violinists). Consequently the stride frequency and the capacity of high frequency cyclic movements are relatively limited in their trainability.

DEVELOPMENT OF MUSCULAR RELAXATION IN SPRINTING

by Aleksandr Goldrin, USSR

An effective sprinting technique depends largely on efficient muscular coordination and, above all, on a relaxed, tension-free running action. In the following text the author presents a variety of drills recommended for the development of coordination and relaxation.

Running, although a basic means of human locomotion, is nevertheless based on a rather complicated coordinated mechanism. Under the term of "coordination" we understand here the harmonious work on the muscles, coordinated by several different nerve cells.

The onset of fatigue and drop in the running speed are often looked at as only the result of exhausted energy sources, overlooking the inhibiting procedsses that occur in the central nervous system. The inhibiting factors in the central nervous system are not only caused by the reduced strength of nerve impulses but also by the frequency (sprinting) and duration (speed endurance) of the impulses.

An effective running technique depends therefore on the relationship of stimulting and inhibiting processes in the brain, expressed in a precise and inductive coordination. This secures in sprinting perfect muscular coordination shown, above all, in a relaxed running action without tension. Consequently, the development of harmonious nervous processes remains the top priority in sprint training.

The system of nervous processes that forms a repetitive stereotype in sprinting must be dynamic and sufficiently flexible to allow for changes when conditions require it. In order to develop a stereotype that corresponds to the dynamics of sprinting it is necessary to employ training runs under different conditions and different tasks. Unfortunately there is not enough emphasis placed on the development of the nervous processes in sprint training, as many coaches believe that relaxed running can simply be achieved through a sufficient training volume.

The following suggestions on how to develop coordination and relaxation are based on different running forms. It must be, however, stressed that the ability to sprint without muscular tension can be developed only with the active participation of the athlete. The responsibility of the coach is the choice of the exercises, based on individual characteristics, level of performance and the athlete's main sprinting distance.

DISTANCE EXERCISES

Inertia Runs

Using the inertia gathered in a full speed sprint distance for a gradually slowing "run-out" is the most common training means to develop relaxation. The athlete, after completing the sprint distance, avoids rapid checking and simply continuous using the inertia for another 50 to 80m. The aim is to avoid any tension and perform the "run-out" completely relaxed.

The most common combinations of this exercise are:

- 30m from a crouch start + 50m relaxed
- 30m with maximal speed from a flying start + 50 to 70m relaxed
- 50m from a crouch start + 100 to 120m without tension.

To evaluate the development of relaxation it is advisable to conduct tests in which equal distances are covered at maximal speed and with inertia. Good relaxation is reflected in small differences between the two runs.

Transition Sprints

Transition sprints consist of 10 to 50m accelerations followed by relaxed transitions with a minimal reduction of speed. The change from fast running to a jog must be smooth with a step by step deceleration. Both the acceleration and transition distances can vary in length. For example: 20 to 30m acceleration + 60 to 100m transition, followed again by an acceleration. The total distance covered in these sprints can range from 200 to 600m. Transition sprints are widely employed as a so called sprint fartlek in cross country conditions.

Acceleration Series

This training means is effectively used by American sprinters. The athlete changes from a jog to a 10 to 40m long tempo run with an emphasized arm action and knee lift. This is followed by a so called "switch off", a change to tension free running in which speed is maintained. A new acceleration follows as soon as the speed begins to drop. The number of repetitions in this type of switching on and off sprints has to be carefully adjusted according to the athlete's performance capacity. Fatigue must be avoided and emphasis is placed on tension free action.

A typical example of this wave-like series is 120m divided into 20m acceleration, 10 to 20m with inertia, 20m acceleration and so on. There are several combinations possible, including 300m distances in 30m acdeleration and 70m with inertia sections. Other variations can be employed by changing the patterns of the transfers to relaxed running and the rate of accelerations.

Varied Speed Runs

It is most common in varied speed sprints to divide the desired distance into three equal sections. The middle section is covered completely relaxed and without tension. For example, if 90m repetitions are performed the middle section is 30m long, for 120m the middle is 40m, for 150m it is 50m and so on. Every effort is made to cover the middle section with a minimal effort and complete relaxation while still trying to maintain the accumulated speed. Timing the middle seciton helps to evaluate the effectiveness of relaxation in comparison to the speed losses.

Once the athlete appears to have succeeded in maintaining speed in a tension free action, the length of the middle section can be increased. For example, 100m divided into 30m + 40m + 30m, or 120m divided into 30m + 60m + 30m.

"Switch-Off" Runs

In the switching off action the elimination of the volititional effort takes place for a few running strides while sprinting at maximal speed. It is recommended for use in the starting acceleration on the curve and in the transition from the forward lean of the start to the normal upright running action.

The athlete has to run with extremely active strides in the start that makes relaxation difficult. Sprinting in the curve is made even more difficult by the task to overcome centrifugal forces. Momentary switching off under these circumstances helps to avoid the development of inhibiting processes in the central nervous system and has a positive influence on the following running action.

The most common variations of the switching off drills are:

- A 30 to 50m starting acceleration, followed by two to four strides without any strain and a rapid change to active running over the next 20 to 30m. It is helpful to have the switch-off point marked
- A 20 to 50m acceleration on the curve, followed by a two to four stride switch-off when entering the straight.
- Full effort 60 to 200m sprints during which the athlete performs several switch-offs signaled by the coach.
- Sprints over 60 to 100m with a switch-off taking place every 10m, 120m sprints with a switch-off every 15m, or 150m sprints with a switch-off every 20m. Here it is again advisable to have the points where the changes to reduced tension occur clearly marked.
- Sprints over 60 to 150m distances with switch-offs on a slight decline, suitable for highly qualified sprinters.

Stride Changes

There are several exercises that help to develop relaxation by employing changes in stride frequency and stride length. Typical examples are as follows:

- Runs over 60 to 100m on a 3 to 5° decline in which each 10 to 20m long section is covered by using different stride frequencies. The sections are marked until the athlete has sufficient experience to decide where the changes have to take place.
- Sprints on a track marked for stride length. The total distance is 30 to 100m with sections of 6 to 10 lines marked for normal stride length, followed by 4 to 6 lines for shorter strides. The performance can take place from a standing or flying start and the aim is to increase running speed.

Falling Forward Starts

A series of falling starts, performed over a distance of 60 to 100m, is another of the many available means to develop relaxation. In this exercise the total distance is divided into marked 10 to 20m long sections. The athlete jogs to the first marker, leans heavily forward with his shoulders and trunk and accelerates sharply to avoid falling.

After performing 6 to 8 accelerating high knee lift strides with a forward lean, the athlete straightens into normal running position and executes the next 6 to 8 strides with maximal relaxation. This is followed by another leaning acceleration and maximal relaxation at each marker until the whole distance has been completed.

Hill Sprints

Selected specific tracks that include uphill and downhill sections provide variety to the development of relaxation through varied tension sprints. In this exercise, performed on a slight decline and incline, the athlete executes a 20 to 30m downhill acceleration, followed by covering the next 20 to 30m on the flat with maximal relaxation. The run is completed with an active 20 to 30m sprint on the uphill section.

Change the Leader

This well known exercise is performed in a group of 4 to 6 athletes who run in a single file 150 to 400m long repetitions. The speed, determined by the coach, is moderate. On the signal from the coach (or the athlete's own initiative) the last runner accelerates and sprints past the other group members to take the leading position. once in the lead, the athlete switches immediately to relaxed, tension free action. A sprint to the front now by the last athlete follows and so on until the planned distance is covered.

The number and the length of the acceleration and relaxation sections depends on the size of the group, the distances between the individual athletes and the length of the whole distance.

Merlene Ottey exhibiting a relaxed, tension-free running action.

28

PERFORMANCE STRUCTURE OF THE 400M AND ITS REALIZATION WITHIN THE COMPLEX METHODS OF TRAINING

by Werner Schafer, German Democratic Republic (in cooperation with Peter Dost)

An analysis of the structural elements of 400m performance, followed by a series of suggestions for the organization of training, based on the complex methods of training and including practical examples.

In order to define more accurately the correlation between speed and endurance in the 400m, it is necessary to take into consideration the competition structure of the long sprint. Looking at the speed pattern over the distance shows that it remains the same for all performance levels, for both men and women (Figure 1).

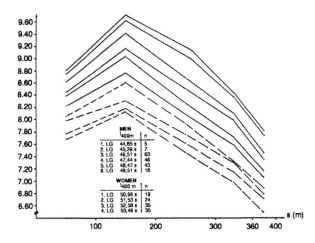

Figure 1: Performance structure of the 400m
(—) MEN (- - -) WOMEN.

It can be seen from the drawing that the velocity curve has three essential features—the acceleration, the maximum running speed and the continuous decline of speed. The performances of better athletes differ accordingly in the overall high speed achieved in all part distances. Thus, an improvement of one second is a complex task as far as training methods are concerned.

The percentage changes in speed in relation to the average racing speed are the same for all performance groups (men and women) (Figure 2).

This means:

1. There is no sex-specific difference between men and women in 400m performance.

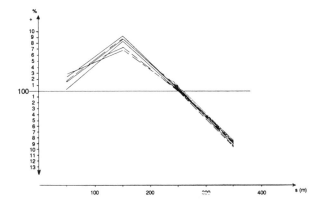

Figure 2: Percentage changes in speed in comparison to average speed in 400m races (men and women) over 100m splits.

Consequently the prerequisites for optimal competitive performance are virtually the same for men and women.

2. The speed pattern in the 400m is clearly determined by the corresponding components of the energy metabolism (Figure 3). The acceleration and the maximal running speed phases are in the alactacid-anaerobic energy metabolism range, which liberates the highest quantity of energy in a time unit, while the locomotor speed endurance is exploited in the lactacid-anaerobic energy phase.

Consequently maximal running speed in the long sprint is already achieved within 40 to 80m of the distance.

This trend indicates that athletes of a higher performance level reach maximal speed earlier than other runners, reducing the time required for acceleration. The decline in speed is, in principle, the same for all performance groups (men and women) and corresponds to about 2.2 to 2.4 seconds for the 200 to 400m section. The maximal racing speed is for this reason a decisive factor.

Thus the speed requirements have a

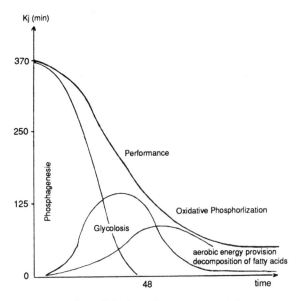

Figure 3: Possibilities of energy provision under maximal demand.

considerable influence on the competitive result. According to our findings, the maximal speed realized in competition is about 90% of the maximal individual locomotor speed capacity (measured during a 30m run from a flying start). The planned competition result can be traced from this.

The influence of the speed requirements increases with the improved performance level. This expresses itself in the correlation between the first and the second 200m section in the 400m race and the final time (Figure 4).

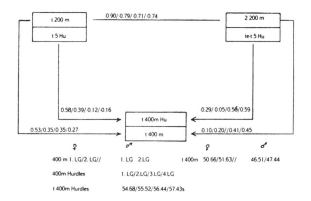

Figure 4: The structure of race performance (400m, 400m hurdles, presented in the first and second 200m for different performance levels.

There is a tendency for an increased influence of the first 200m section on the final time when the performance level improves. It appears in concrete terms that a 0.87 second improvement for women is achieved by a 58.6% (0.51 sec.) reduction of the first 200m and a 41.4% reduction of the second 200m.

The ratio for a 0.93 second improvement for men is 54.8% (0.51 sec.) to 45.2% (0.42 sec.).

The sample correlations of the four groups of women's 400m hurdlers show clearly that there is a reversal in the significance that the two halves of the distance have on the final time when the performance level of an athlete improves. This is to be borne in mind in the development of young athletes in the long sprint.

An increased development of specific endurance in comparison to other training means leads young athletes relatively quickly to results corresponding to lower performance groups (also in respect to personal best performances). This is often shown in junior championships. Those winning or being placed in the 400m are frequently also winners and placegetters in the 800m, but virtually never in the 100m.

This premature adoption of specific endurance training is, as a rule, associated with a neglect of speed development. It results in the closing of a straight path to better performances and leads to stagnation in the 400m, often even to a change to different running events.

High negative correlation coefficients are noticeable in the two part distances in competition runs. They show that the faster the first 200m is covered, the slower is the second 200m. This means that the second 200m can be covered relatively faster only if the first 200m hasn't been too fast. This is a well-known fact in practice. However, it is essential to cover also the first 200m at a high speed for international top-level performance. This is only possible when the speed qualifications of the athlete are sufficiently high for a reserve margin. World-class performances therefore require speed capacities above those expressed in maximal race speed. Accordingly, the performance achieved in the second 200m, which is the decisive factor for winning, depends largely on the capacities that decide the performance of the first 200m. It follows from this that no decisive 400m improvement can be achieved by placing a one-sided emphasis on the development of specific endurance over 300 to 500m distances. It can easily lead to the neglect of the development of the prerequisites for the first 200m (strength/speed).

Looking at the lactate-performance relationship, and the possibility of improved performance derived from it, confirms this hypothesis.

According to Pansold, et. al., the lactate-performance relationship is determined by three key values: the aerobic performance capacity (VL_4), the pattern of increase (b) and the blood lactate concentration (Figure 5), in which the nature of the

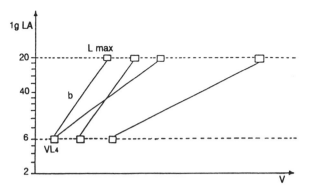

Figure 5: Possible increased performance assuming the same maximal blood lactate concentration.

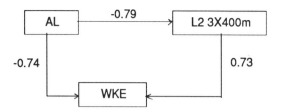

Figure 6: The influence of aerobic performance capacity of athlete (AL) on the race performance (WKE) and the quality of specific training (L2 3x400m).

increase (b) expresses the development level of individual strength capacities for the complex strength/locomotor speed requirements of the long sprint.

A shift of the lactate-performance relationship to the right, and with it an improved performance, is therefore achieved through an improvement in the complex strength-speed and the aerobic capacity. The individual maximum blood lactate concentration, on the other hand, appears to be a necessary condition that by itself does not produce an improved performance.

In clearly different performances (49.02 to 58.30), for example, Koch and another athlete had the same maximal blood lactate concentration (20.6 mmol/l) after the race. However, there were important differences between the two athletes in their speed capacities (2.90 seconds against 3.53 seconds in the flying 30m), clearly responsible for the difference in their performances.

The lactate-performance relationship in the long sprint shows a deviation to the left and with it a declined performance when training emphasis is based on one-sided alactacid specific endurance and the development of strength/speed capacities, as well as aerobic endurance, is overlooked. These two capacities represent therefore a fundamental prerequisite for the development of the competition performance and must be developed all year round.

The same is true for aerobic capacity, which up to now has received little attention. We can prove the effect of the aerobic capacity on the competition results (a better competition result requires a higher aerobic capacity), as well as on the quality of specific training. The higher quality of specific training, in turn, has a strong influence on competition results (Figure 6). This knowledge was responsible for the considerable development of our long sprinters.

Endurance runs, because they can be easily

guided, have recently proven to be the most effective means of developing aerobic capacity. There are, however, other training measures, such as prolonged warm-up and warm-down runs, or the use of bicycle ergometers, that have an aerobic effect.

Schönlebe, for example, employed for the development of aerobic capacity endurance runs over 8 to 10km in a training unit. In principle it is considered unnecessary to use longer endurance runs (for example, 15km).

The control of the running speed takes place over a standard distance in the aerobic-anaerobic transition range (lactate 2 to 4 mmol/l). The number of training units per week in the phase of the development of basic capacities should be 5 to 6, in the phase of specific build-up 3 to 4 and in the phase of a series of competitions 2 to 3.

The development of the aerobic capacity of Schönlebe's over a year and over several years is presented in Figure 7. It shows that:

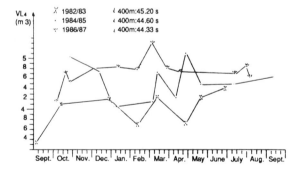

Figure 7: The multi-year development of aerobic capacity of athletes.

1. It is necessary to maintain a high aerobic level throughout the year, not merely on single occasions.

2. The available aerobic performance capacity can be subject to relatively large short-term fluctuations. This occurs mainly when training measures employed for its development have been neglected or lactacid specific training is undertaken

**Thomas Schönlebe, GDR,
1987 400m World Champion**

performance has not turned out to be the case.

Specific performance capacity can be brought to the required level only by the highly complex interaction of the training means employed. This can be illustrated by the example of Schönlebe's first preparation period in the year 1987/88. He set up at the end of this period a world 400m indoor record of 45.05 seconds and reached a corresponding 20.93 seconds in the 200m distance. The following essential features should be noted:

1. The initial performances at the start of the year had dropped only slightly in comparison to the best performances in the previous year. This allowed training to begin at a relatively high level. Compared with the previous year:

- the maximal locomotor speed was   96.9%
- the maximal strength was   100.0%
- the aerobic performance capacity was   95.1%

2. A good aerobic and total muscular support was available for the development of specific endurance. Schönlebe covered in the first 10 weeks 362km and the next five weeks 147km in endurance runs. His aerobic capacity in the 10th week after the start of trianing was 4.80m/sec. (VL_4) and in the 15th week 4.90m/sec. More than 13 hours a week in the first 10 weeks and more than 8 hours a week in the following weeks was spent on the development of general athletic capacities.

3. There was a close link between strength training and speed training.

A striking feature in the strength training was the large volume of event specific power endurance training (jumps, weights) that was closely related to the long intensity runs for specific endurance (400 to 500m). It reached the peak (818 repetitions) in the fourth week after the start of training. This was later continued with 600 to 650 repetitions until two weeks prior to a competition. The event specific power and strength endurance training was linked with a calculated volume of acceleration and speed training, making up about 50%. Long acceleration runs (up to 60m) continued to make up around 55% of the overall total of acceleration training. The acceleration runs and particularly the long runs represents an important link between power and strength endurance training with speed training.

Two independent training complexes have emerged from the analysis of the training structure and the performance in the long sprint. They are relatively independent of one another, but form an inseparable unity, whereby each of these complexes is developed by their own training measures (Figure 8).

The link between these complexes is established

in large volumes. A particular example of this is the training in sub-maximal speed range.

3. The use of endurance runs for aerobic development is therefore possible and also necessary in the phases of specific training and series of competitions. The endurance runs have here a strong compensating effect and represent no additional risk to the heavily loaded muscle groups, tendons and ligaments.

4. The often expressed fear that endurance running will have a negative effect on speed

by the medium length runs (as a rule 300m). Obviously this is only then effective when the linked complexes themselves show a high level of development. This link was made in a training unit of extremely high intensity (300m in 32.7/32.2 sec./400m in 44.8 sec., hand timed) in the first preparation period in 1987/88. It was followed a week later by the world indoor record.

During the specific sub-maximal training phase there was a ratio of 2:1 between the speed oriented complex and the complex of specific endurance. That is, every 2km of speed oriented training corresponded to 1km of specific endurance training.

The speed oriented complex during the preparation period is, as a rule, more intensive than that of specific endurance training. Intensity has absolute priority over the volume in the speed oriented complex of training, while the priority in the specific endurance training complex must definitely be on the volume.

Figure 8: Diagram of the specific performance structure in the 400m run.

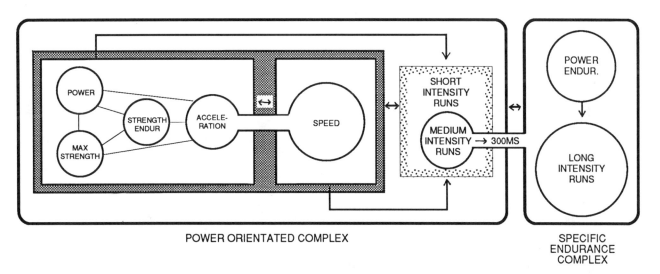

POWER ORIENTATED COMPLEX   SPECIFIC ENDURANCE COMPLEX

BASIC RESTORATION PROCEDURES—A SUMMARY

by M. Zallessky, V. Sobolevsky and L. Khomenov, USSR

The following article is a summary of Soviet views on the basic principles of restoration, covering natural and artificial measures recommended to restore the physical and mental performance capacities of an athlete.

It is a well known fact that training loads have to be gradually increased in order to develop the required performance capacities. This can be achieved effectively by observing the following principles:

- The level reached in physical development of an athlete must be taken into consideration.
- There should be a gradual transition to higher training loads.
- A well-planned complex of contemporary training methods must be employed.
- Training should take place under the guidance of qualified coaches and medical advisers.
- Effective means of restoration must be employed.

The finding and application of effective means of restoration presents one of the most important problems in contemporary track and field, as restoration cannot be looked at as simply having adequate rest. On the contrary, it means the employment of proper recovery methods to restore the functional capacites after single loads within a training session, beween training sessions and between series of workouts. This can be achieved by using artificial, as well as natural restoration methods.

The artificial methods usually include different forms of soft massage, sauna, steam baths, various water treatments, auto-suggestive rest and pharmacological means. The natural methods, allowing the body to restore itself, are based on creating the best possible conditions for recovery through well planned coaching that takes into consideration individual needs. This means the designing and application of individual training plans that achieve the optimal relationship between work loads and the athlete's performance capacities.

NATURAL MEANS

Once a Day Training

Looking at athletes who train only once a day shows that a 24-hour interval between training sessions can provide complete restoration. In this case a planned training load can be used for a long time period. A typical example of this is the up to six month long preparation period of distance runners. No passive rest days are employed in this situation and restoration takes place by reduced training loads at certain intervals.

The reduced loads occur usually on one or two days in each microcycle (7 days), followed by a restoration week after two or three heavy microcycles. A significantly reduced work load is applied in the restoration week to create a high compensation effect. During the competition season these restoration periods can be extended to a fortnight prior to important meetings, provided this phase follows maximal physical and psychological training loads.

It is important that the training and competition microcycles produce a positive shift of adaption processes, achieved through an effective alteration of training loads and restoration periods. This should take place in a wave-like pattern of work and recovery in which the changes of work loads and restorations are moving gradually upwards. The crests of the waves move higher but the curves of the waves vary in length, according to the number of training sessions conducted with the same load.

Several Daily Sessions

Restoration procedures become a little more complicated when athletes train two or three times a day. In this case it is important in natural restoration to establish a correct and efficient sequence of the training sessions. Usually, the morning workouts, in which light loads are employed, play a preparatory role for the main training session. The evening workouts, on the other hand, are designed for restoration purposes.

For this reason the evening sessions in three times a day training do not include much specialized work but take more or less the format of active rest, made up of games and exercises that allow restoration of the functional capacities of the central nervous system. For example, sprint training is followed by a game of basketball or volleyball.

In a twice a day training program the main workouts combine the major tasks with active rest type of restoration activities. The same routine is also applied to macrocycles, in which the recovery cycles are incorporated in the program following a certain number of heavily loaded microcycles. These active rest transition phases must ensure that the nervous system can recover while physical work continues.

It must be kept in mind that restoration during these phases takes place regardless of the intensity of training. However, long duration of intense physical activity is to be avoided, as it can otherwise lead to decreased physical performance capacities. The key factor is to avoid fatigued situations and take the load off the central nervous system.

OTHER FACTORS

Running in the country is regarded as a very effective active rest type of restoration method in many situations. These very low intensity runs are excellent for recovery after intense training sessions, as well as after competitions. They can also be recommended at the first signs of overtraining if preventive methods, such as up to three days of active rest at the end of a training cycle, have failed to produce the desired results. In less drastic circumstances restoration can be achieved by employing reduced training loads, short of what was planned for a particular training cycle.

It is known that repetitive specific training intensifies the possibility of overtraining and reduces the restoration effects. This can be avoided by the introduction of variations to the training methods that achieve the same specific results. Selected jumping exercises, for example, can replace jumping over the bar in the high jump.

However, the choice of training exercises for variety must be based on means and methods that have a positive mental influence.

This would not only improve the restoration of the athlete's work capacity but would also allow the introduction of more frequent active restoration phases. Preference in this situation must be given to training means that are close to the specific demands of an event to ensure that the training effect does not suffer.

Relaxation exercises, performed in a training session between training loads, play an important part in restoration. These exercises are often followed by the use of passive rest, although this occurs mainly at the end of a training session. The passive rest can include the use of autosuggestion to improve relaxation. It can also be employed successfully in between very heavy training loads in a workout, provided the load is decreased before the passive rest takes place.

Exercises for relaxation, combined with deep breathing and walking, make up another effective method of active restoration in the last part of a training session and after competitions. Coaches are advised to make more use of this type of restoration in the warm-down periods.

Finally, it should be noted that a well executed warm-up plays a role in restoration. A good warm-up assures that the athlete has reached an optimal mental and physical state to perform the planned work, which in turn guarantees more effective restoration processes between single loads in a training session.

ARTIFICIAL MEANS

The main artificial restoration methods, such as massage, vibromassage, steam baths, sauna, different water treatments, electrostimulation, pressure chambers and others, provide additional valuable assistance in recovery. These methods can be divided into two categories, means that have general physical effect and means with relatively more effect locally.

The most common general means include massage, baths in combination with other water treatments, sauna and so on. Local procedures make use of local massage, limbs placed in pressure chambers, heating, electrostimulation and so on. Athletes who train two or three times a day are advised to employ local procedures in between each workout and general methods at the end of the day. General methods are also recommended after large volumes of work, while local methods follow small volumes and local loads in training.

A complex use of the various artificial restoration measures takes place during the highest training load periods and during the competition season. This includes general procedures in massage, underwater massage, different types of baths and saunas, as well as several local effect methods, such as the pressure chamber, heating and electrostimulation.

Whatever artificial methods of restoration are employed, it is important to understand that the recovery effect of one or another of these begins to decline with long use, as the body adapts itself to the treatment. It is therefore best to employ the above mentioned complexes of several methods and to use the same restricted means only one or two days in a microcycle.

Artificial restoration measures include, in addition to those already listed, pharmacological aids and physiotherapy. Both methods and their dosages are usually worked out with the help of a doctor. Medical advice is needed when it is necessary to consider the possibility of using pharmacological preparations to improve recovery in the restorative system. The same advice is advisable for physiotherapy measures, particularly when an athlete is susceptible to injuries.

It is generally recommended that physiotherapy procedures take place an hour after the end of a training session or about $1^{1}/_{2}$ hours after dinner. The therapy sessions last about 30 to 40 minutes and must be completed at least 30 mintues before the following training session begins. Physiotherapy is often combined with other general and local restoration procedures.

All artificial restoration measures are normally reduced in the microcycles leading to competitions. In the use of local effect procedures, it is advisable to employ these every second day, placing special emphasis on massage. From the general procedures sauna is used only once a week and not later than four days before a competition. During the tapering microcycle all other general restoration procedures are employed to the fullest extent.

IN CONCLUSION

An aspect often overlooked in restoration is the fact that the effects of training and recovery can be considerably improved by making use of different facilities and training venues. These changes not only have psychological influence, but also allow an increase in the training volume. The change of venues, making use of woods, parks, grass surfaces and so on, helps to reduce the load on the skeletal-muscular system and increases the restorative capabilities of the body. Positive psychological recovery processes are achieved by providing different environments at the changing training venues.

Finally, whatever the measures employed, restoration depends to a great extent on the functional capacity levels of an athlete and the significance of solid physical preparation is not to be overlooked. It is a known fact that restorative processes occur faster and more efficiently as the performance capacities of an athlete improve. In other words, the higher the performance level, the quicker the recovery.

ENERGY SYSTEMS AND THE 400M RACE

by Kevin Pendergast, Australia

Success in the 400m depends not only on basic speed but also on a wise utilization of the four energy systems that are triggered at different speeds. The following text looks at the four systems and the distribution of energy over the 400m distance.

Muscular contraction causes all movements by rotating a limb about a joint. This contraction is caused by a substance known as adenosine triphosphate, usually abbreviated to ATP. No ATP, no contraction, no contraction, no movement. There are four sources for ATP, and these are the four energy systems. All are used intensively in a 400m race.

ENERGY SYSTEMS

The energy systems are the means and the fuels for producing ATP. They differ in their ability to produce power (the time rate of doing work) and in their capacity (the total energy which can be produced).

Aerobic Energy System

As its name suggests, this system works on burning a fuel in the presence of oxygen to produce energy. In this case the fuel is glycogen, a carbohydrate stored in the muscle, and the energy produced enables adenosine diphosphate (ADP) to combine with free phosphorous to form ATP in a high energy bond. The ATP enables the muscle to contract by releasing the energy from the bond and the ATP breaks down again to ADP and free phosphorous. The ADP and the phosphorous can combine again to form ATP and the process can continue as long as oxygen and glycogen are available. (A qualification which only applies to marathon runners is that fat and protein can be used when glycogen has been depleted). The process is depicted graphically in Figure 1.

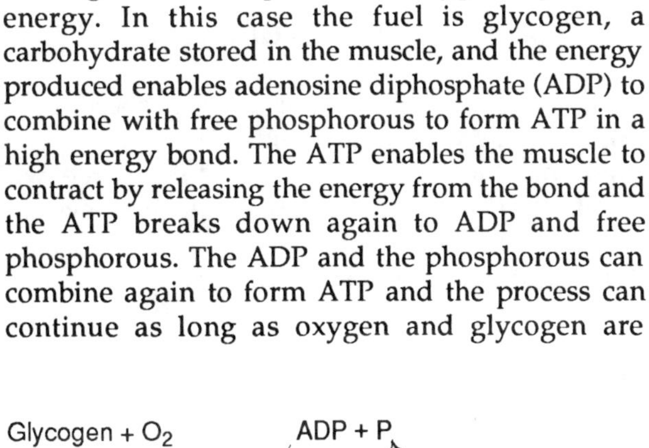

This is a steady-state system and is limited by the rate of oxygen intake and consumption. It is the most efficient of the systems and can continue for a long period until the fuel sources are depleted. It is the system most easily activated and comes into play for gentle contractions. However, it is also the least powerful of the energy systems. For instance, world class distance runners, who rely almost entirely on the aerobic system, run at little more than 6 meters per second, whereas world class sprinters average more than 10 meters per second and peak at above 11 meters per second. When oxygen intake is insufficient to provide the speed required, another energy system must be called upon. Obviously the greater the capacity to take in and consume oxygen, the faster will be the steady-state speed, and the less reliance on the more powerful systems.

Lactic Anaerobic System

Anaerobic indicates without oxygen and is called upon when the oxygen system cannot deliver sufficient speed. Glycogen burns without oxygen to produce the energy which enables ADP and phosphorous to combine to form ATP. This process produces ATP faster than the aerobic system and is therefore more powerful, but unfortunately at a cost. The breakdown of glycogen without oxygen produces lactic acid, which inhibits the functioning of the muscle.

The faster the pace the more rapid the production of the acid, which accumulates in the muscle and will not be dispersed until after

Glycogen + O_2 → Energy → ADP + P → Energy → Muscular Contraction

CO_2 + H_2O → ATP

Figure 1: The process of the aerobic energy system.

strenuous effort ceases. Therefore the lactic anaerobic effort is necessarily one of deceleration. The speed is reduced until it reaches a level which can be sustained by the aerobic system. The process is depicted in Figure 2.

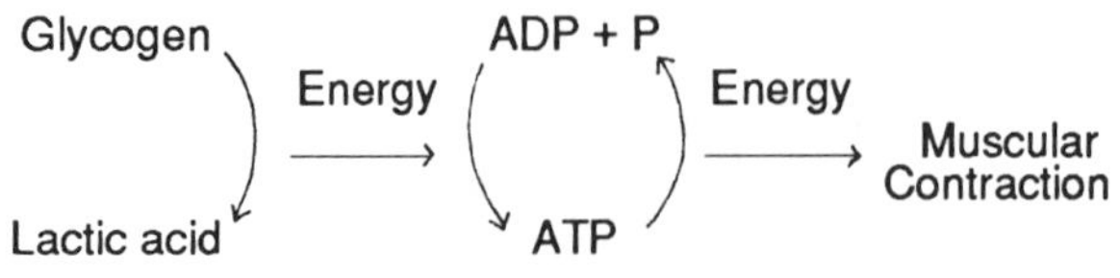

Glycogen, ADP + P
) Energy ( ) Energy
Lactic acid' → ( ) → Muscular Contraction
            ↘ ATP ⁄

Figure 2: The process of the lactic anaerobic system.

It takes from 30 minutes to one hour for a large accumulation of lactic acid to dissipate, which is the reason why quality performances lasting longer than 30 seconds cannot be repeated inside about one hour. The limiting factors in the lactic anaerobic system are the ability to produce lactic acid and the ability to tolerate it.

Alactic Anaerobic System

This system works without oxygen and without producing lactic acid. A high energy substance, creatin phosphate (CP), breaks down into creatin and phosphorous, and the energy released enables ADP and free phosphorous to combine to form ATP. Later, when ATP is freely available from the aerobic system, it provides energy for the recreation of CP. The power available from this system is greater than from either the aerobic or lactic anaerobic systems.

However, power is the rate of expending energy and the CP system is like a big tap—high output, but it empties the tank quickly. There is not much CP in the tank, enough for about 5 seconds at maximum effort. This system is stimulated when the demand is great; it is not called upon at lower speeds. The process is depicted in Figure 3.

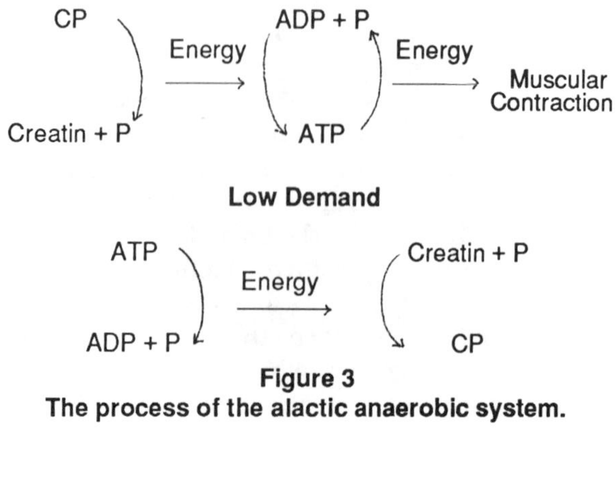

High Demand

CP, ADP + P
) Energy ( ) Energy
Creatin + P' → ( ) → Muscular Contraction
            ↘ ATP ⁄

Low Demand

ATP, / Creatin + P
) Energy (
ADP + P ⁄ ↘ CP

Figure 3
The process of the alactic anaerobic system.

Most stocks of CP are replenished within 2 to 3 minutes of the termination of the exercise. This is the reason why an athlete can perform bursts of 30 to 40m with only a few minutes recoveries between the repetitions.

The limiting factors of the alactic anaerobic system are the amount of CP in the muscle and the ability to utilize it. There is a small amount of ATP stored in the muscle, but it is only enough for about one second of an intense effort. In other words, for a runner it is only useful for the start, perhaps only the initial thrust with each leg. It does not really enter into consideration in planning the distribution of effort and will not be considered here.

Speed Triggers

The aerobic and the two anaerobic systems are all triggered at different speeds. According to the literature and the author's own analysis of performances at different levels, the triggering of speeds, in comparison to the 100m speed, is graphically presented in Figure 4.

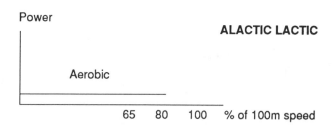

Figure 4
The triggering of energy systems at different speeds.

DISTRIBUTION OF ENERGY

Success in 400m depends on basic speed, but it also depends on wise utilization of the energy systems. Inattention to any of the three will inhibit performance. Of course, all three systems have to be trained and this will be covered later. Suffice to say at this stage that your preparation to date has trained all three. However, training alone is not enough. The systems have to be used intelligently in a race, where everything hinges mainly on the use of the alactic system.

Suppose you decide to save yourself as much as possible so that you can accelerate home. You do this by saving the alactic system until the last 100m. If you run 100m in 11 seconds, that means you cover first 300m in 41.3 seconds at best, leaving you 8.7 seconds for the last 100m to achieve 50 seconds.

On the other hand (still an 11-second 100m runner), you decide to set yourself up with a fast first 200m. You run close to flat out, say 22.5 seconds, which would certainly deplete your CP stocks. The fastest you could run after that would be at the rate of 13.75 seconds, per 100m, i.e., 27.5 seconds for the last 200m, which would give you 50 seconds for the 400m. However, remember that the last 200m now uses the lactic system which is necessarily decelerating. In fact, to run the first 200m in 22.5 seconds, you would have been well into your lactic system and the lactic acid would already be accumulating at the 200m mark. By the time you reached the finish you would be down to your aerobic system, i.e., 16.9 seconds, per 100m pace. Assuming a linear deceleration, you would run 30.4 seconds for the last 200m, giving you a 400m time of 52.9 seconds.

Obviously the aim must be to string the alactic system out as long as possible. We don't know the precise relationship between running speed and the rate of the use of CP, but we can make some interpolations and intelligent guesses.

A reasonable first estimate would be that the optimal speed would be 90% of 100m speed, i.e., 12.22 seconds 100m pace for the first part of the race. This is halfway between no alactic system and the alactic system at its maximum output. We don't know whether this could be maintained for all of the race but, if it could, it would lead to a time of 48.9 seconds. One factor indicates that it could not be maintained—nobody does it. No top 400m run is ever covered at constant speed. It is unlikely that they are all wrong. A factor against constant speed being the optimum strategy is that it under-utilizes the lactic system—there is no deceleration. If the first 200m is run at 90%, the second is likely to slip to about 85%, i.e., 25.9 seconds, giving a 400m time of 50.3 seconds.

A reasonable second estimate would be that the optimal speed would be 95% of the 100m speed, i.e., an 11.6 second 100m pace for the first 200m. This would give a first 200m of 23.2 seconds and, being reasonably gentle for a 22-second 200m runner, would not completely tax the alactic system. However, the CP source would be diminishing and the lactic system would be contributing more and more, with a consequent buildup of lactic acid and the inevitable deceleration. Good 400m runners are at about 80% of their 100m speed at the end of the race, i.e., just at the end of the alactic zone. The deceleration from 95% to 80% indicates a second 200m of about 87.5% of the 100m speed, i.e., 25.1 seconds. This would give a 400m time of 48.3 seconds, which seems reasonable for a 400m runner who can run 11

seconds for the 100m. The differential between the first and second 200's is 1.9 seconds which is within the 1.5 to 2.0 seconds range seen in all good 400m performances.

The above analysis applies to all 400m runners, although the percentage speeds are typical only to the sprinters. A middle distance type athlete, while short of the 100m speed of a sprinter, can run closer to his maximum for longer. He has a better developed lactic system and also is better trained in extending his alactic system. Consequently, if he is capable of a 23.0 second 200m, he could run at 97.5% for the first 200m for 23.6 seconds and at 92.5% for the second 200m for 24.8 seconds. This would give a time of 48.4 seconds, about the same as the above described athlete.

In summary:

	1st 200	2nd 200	
Sprinter	95%	87.5%	of 100m speed
Middle Distance Type	97.5%	92.5%	of 100m speed

Darren Clark, Australia's 1990 Commonwealth Games 400m Champion

CHAPTER II:
TRAINING PROCEDURES

DEVELOPING AND MAINTAINING MAXIMUM SPEED IN SPRINTS OVER ONE YEAR

by Frank Dick, Great Britain

The development of maximum speed rests on establishing a sound technical model and improving the relevant physical capacities. In this text the author looks at the key techniques in sprinting in order to develop and maintain maximum speed.

The Discipline

To the winner of the Olympic 100m goes the accolade "The world's fastest man/woman". It is a discipline where the focus of achievement in terms of improved performance and/or in terms of defeating opponents is measured in tiny time increments: increments of performance improvement may be as small as 1/100th seconds; while the difference between a gold and silver medal may require examination of photo finish detail to 1/100th seconds.

In preparing an athlete to challenge performance standards and opposition in eventual pursuit of Olympic success, the coach has rejected the old adage that "sprinters are born not made". Instead he has considered the needs of the athlete against the demands of the discipline; evaluated potential contribution of all relevant resources; then prepared custom built programs designed to meet short, medium and long term objectives.

The Discipline Sections

The demands of the discipline might be understood by considering the five sections of the 100m:

a) Reaction and Response Speed=Reaction time and 10m time
b) Starting Accelerations =30m time
c) Pick-up Acceleration=Distance required to achieve maximum speed
d) Maintaining Maximum Speed=Distance maximum speed held
e) Reducing the rate of loss of maximum speed=Distance over which near maximum is held after maximum speed peak is passed.

10m Breakdown in Seoul Finals

To illustrate these, we should look at the data made available by the IAAF Biomechanical Analysis program from the Seoul Olympic 100m finals. (See next page, bottom.)

As a), b) and c) are dealt with by Bob Inglis, brief comment on these sections is made here:

a) The 10m performances for the first three men show that the pattern of the race for them was being laid down very early. The difference between the first three women's 10m performances was rather less significant.
b) The men's 30m times clearly separate Johnson from the field, 0.10 seconds was sufficient difference for Lewis to be aware of Johnson's lead and what this meant. It should be born in mind that from this point onwards, the data should not be read simply as a series of sprinting speed measures, but as products of the complex process of athletes expressing their techniques aware of the challenges of the opposition.
c) The final phase of acceleration would appear, from the data presented here, to bring athletes to maximum speed in the 50m and 60m section of the run—except in the case of Griffith Joyner. We shall consider this phase further here.
d) For every athlete, except Griffith Joyner, maximum speed was maintained for one 10m section. If we consider as maximum speed "fastest 10m time and fastest 10m time + 0.01 seconds", we have varying profiles:

JOHNSON		LEWIS		CHRISTIE	
40-50m	0.84			40m-50m	0.85
50m-60m	0.83	50m-60m	0.83	50m-60m	0.84
60m-70m	0.84				

GRIFFITH JOYNER		ASHFORD		DRECHSLER	
50m-60m	0.92	50m-60m	0.96	50m-60m	0.94
60m-70m	0.91	60m-70m	0.95	60m-70m	0.95
70m-80m	0.91	70m-80m	0.95	70m-80m	0.95
80m-90m	0.91	70m-80m	0.95	70m-80m	0.95
90m-100m	0.92				

It is my opinion that the capacity to maintain a speed within 0.01 seconds of maximum for 30m should be the object of the sprinters. Lewis' mid-race data reflects a loss of concentration rather than a fair picture of his capacity to hold maximum speed:

40m-50m	0.86
50m-60m	0.83
60m-70m	0.85

Griffith Joyner's data suggests that here maximum speed was not achieved in this race. She in fact held a speed within 0.02 seconds of her fastest 10m time in the Seoul Olympic Finals for the final 60m of the race!

e) There is difficulty in drawing conclusions from the available data in reference to Johnson and Lewis. There had been so much publicity surrounding the Johnson-Lewis encounter since Rome, that the two sprinters viewed themselves as the only two probable winners. They ran the race against each other rather than all 8 finalists. By 70m Johnson had reached his maximum 0.16 seconds lead over Lewis—and held this to 80m after which point Johnson ran the final 20m as if the race had already been won (arms aloft for the final 10m); and Lewis ran as if he'd lost. Thus, Johnson covered the final 10m 0.07 seconds slower. As for Griffith Joyner—she was still within 0.01 seconds of her fastest 10m in the race, again raising the question whether or not she had achieved her maximum speed.

This leaves Christie, Ashford and Drechsler. The drop off from maximum speed to the finish was:

Christie	0.04 seconds
Ashford	0.02 seconds
Drechsler	0.03 seconds

From this and other data, it would appear that 0.02-0.04 is the normal range.

100m MEN'S FINAL

	Johnson		Lewis		Christie	
10	1.83		1.89		1.92	
20	2.87	1.04	2.96	1.07	2.97	1.05
30	3.80	.93	3.90	.94	3.92	.95
40	4.66	.86	4.79	.89	4.81	.89
50	5.50	.84	5.65	.86	5.66	.85
60	6.33	.83	6.48	.83	6.50	.84
70	7.17	.84	7.33	.85	7.36	.86
80	8.02	.85	8.18	.85	8.22	.86
90	8.89	.87	9.04	.86	9.09	.87
100	9.79	.90	9.92	.88	9.97	.88

100m WOMEN'S FINAL

	Griffith Joyner		Ashford		Drechsler	
10	2.00		2.02		2.01	
20	3.09	1.09	3.13	1.11	3.12	1.11
30	4.09	1.00	4.15	1.02	4.14	1.02
40	5.04	.95	5.11	.96	5.11	.97
50	5.97	.93	6.07	.97	6.08	.97
60	6.89	.92	7.01	.94	7.02	.94
70	7.80	.91	7.96	.95	7.97	.95
80	8.71	.91	8.91	.95	8.92	.95
90	9.62	.91	9.87	.96	9.88	.96
100	10.54	.92	10.83	.96	10.85	.97

Coaching 100m

In coaching sprinters for the 100m, the coach seeks to prepare the athlete for the demands of each of these five sections—and for blending these into a whole. He must also, of course, build into the program, either through training or through competition itself, preparation for head to head competition.

The broad framework of preparation assumes a simple shape.

Phase 1: Develop basic conditioning
  • all round balanced strength
  • sound general mobility
  • running endurance
  • general speed of coordination

Phase 2: Develop basic sprint technique(s)
  • driving
  • striding
  • lifting

Phase 3: Develop specific conditioning
  • specific strength
  • specific endurance
  • specific speed of coordination
  • specific mobility

Phase 4: Develop advanced technique(s)
  • driving
  • striding
  • lifting
  • race experience/tactics

Stride and Lift Techniques as the Basis of Sprint Development

In former times the basis of selecting sprinters was, in the first instance, results in age group sprint races. Unfortunately, many high potential sprinters were lost at this point because too often age group sprinting success is determined by starting efficiency!

Although times and wins continue to be of interest to coaches, there is increasing awareness that central to all sprints development is a sound sprint striding technique. As a consequence, coaches now place much greater early emphasis on ensuring that the athlete is exposed to a relevant conditioning program of the sprint stride. The other two sprint techniques are built around this.

At a time, then, when much is made of specific conditioning and coordination drills, there is growing emphasis in ensuring that the first two phases (above) are more carefully dealt with in the athletes development at all levels.

When considering maximum speed, the focus of attention on technique shifts from the driving technique of sections a + b through the striding technique of c to the lifting techniques of d then the striding techniques of e.

The lifting technique is normally only a feature of the experienced athletes "armory", but it can be introduced to the developing athlete's technique training program. It is used as the athlete reaches the point of maximum speed—when coordination balances precariously on the brink of risk. The foot contact is at its priviest. As momentum catapults the body past each contact, that contact must contribute to the momentum. To keep contact for even a millisecond too long in trying to express strength will bring loss of speed. The focus is lightness of touch and coordination at speed.

It requires a foundation of specific strength, mobility and endurance—and mastery of the stride technique. Above all, it requires control. Without doubt, like all techniques, it must be practiced. However, the difficulty is that if the athletes must endure the exhausting experience of maximal accelerations in order to reach maximum speed—the number of repetitions of runs at maximum speed to rehearse lifting and/or striding at this pace or at near to this pace, will be seriously restricted. Consequently to practice maximum speed.

Because sound technique—both striding and lifting—are critical to development of maximum speed, their key features are worth review.

STRIDING

Posture: The athlete has the appearance of "Running Tall," shoulders are down, not hunched.

There should be an impression of trunk strength. The whole movement should be smooth and continuous—not jerky and broken.

Arms: **MEN**

Elbow angle of approximately 90° is held. A full range of action is pursued—with the elbow pulled back and high with a strong "squeeze".

The hand reaches shoulder height on the forward beat—and the hip on the backward beat.

WOMEN

a) High stride frequency—coordination emphasis. Elbow angle of approximately 90° is held.

A short, fast "drum beating" action—mostly in front of the body.

b) "New generation" high hip/leg

complex strength emphasis. Arm action as for men.

Legs: The athlete strikes the ground with a claw-like action from a high knee lift. Women a) technique athletes do not have as high a knee lift as a women b) a full range of action is pursued.

LIFTING

Posture: As for striding, there should be an overall impression of lightness and speed of knee lift.

Arms: The arm action is similar to that of the stride technique. The main difference is a slight increase in the speed of action.

The range is virtually the same, but for a more emphatic pumping/beating in front of the body. The women a) is, in effect, a more exaggerated version of the "stride technique" arms.

Legs: The leg action is characterized by a higher, faster knee lift or "prancing". It is a light, fast movement associated with a quicker, more active, and lighter striking/clawing motion of the foot. It is as if it is the track which is speeding under the athlete—and the foot as only the briefest of moments to match this speed and touch it at that speed.

The women a) technique athletes find problems with the concept of a higher knee lift—and resolve the problem simply by maintaining a very high frequency of striding.

DEVELOPMENT OF MAXIMUM SPEED

Athletes working to develop the maximum speed sections of 100m, must include certain specific training units throughout the annual cycle. While there clearly are several ways of designing relevant programs—all pursue similar principles.

(i) Specific strength units are included through the annual cycle but are reduced or removed during competition phases.

(ii) Strength units for women are continued later than men's—well into the competition phase.

(iii) Sub-maximum to maximum technique work is incorporated within each microcycle throughout the annual cycle as a means of relating conditioning work to technique development.

(iv) Specific maximum speed work to supermaximum speed work is mainly restricted to precompetition and competition phases, but can be located in specific preparation blocks of work where altitude, elastic catapult, downhill sprints or supermaximal speed treadmills, etc. are used.

(v) All systems use a double periodized year. Moreover, the various training units of systems enjoy certain common characteristics:

(i) Specific strength work uses interplay between relevant muscle dynamics and joint action.

(ii) Where high intensity strength loadings are a feature of the program (90-100%), units can be continued through even to the days of competition.

(iii) Initially there is progression from sub-maximum to maximum speed intra unit and inter unit, to ensure the integrity of techniques.

(iv) When working at maximum or super maximum speeds there are full recoveries with stimulus duration of 2.0 seconds-3.0 seconds—in sets of 2-4 and repetitions of 2-4. Athletes build gradually to maximum speed—rapid accelerations are avoided. Units for maximum speeds development are normally separated by 48 hours. Two units per weekly microcycle are sufficient where other units include starts, acceleration and pick up work.

(v) Maximum speed work, accelerations, starting or pick up—all are performed with squads—and not by an athlete on his/her own.

(vi) The high intensity nature of training demands that regeneration units are liberally distributed through the competition and competition microcycle. It is also essential that athletes have access to a comprehensive program of medical management.

(vii) Coaches use personally devised tables for contrasts of strength, speed and speed endurance. For example—I use the following (Tables 1 and 2, next page).

AN INTERPRETATION OF PROGRAM DETAIL FOR MAXIMUM SPEED DEVELOPMENT

In practical terms—one interpretation of these common principles and characteristics is as follows:

Table 1: Controls for 100m/200m athletes

Time Trials — hand timed						Competition Performance (electric timing)	
30m from Blocks	30m Flying	60m from Blocks	150m from Standing*	250m from Standing*	60m	100m	200m
3.58-3.61	2.48-2.51	6.22-6.27	14.87-14.97	25.47-25.72	6.49-6.53	10.09-10.16	20.17-20.32
3.62-3.65	2.52-2.55	6.28-6.33	14.98-15.08	25.73-25.98	6.54-6.58	10.17-10.24	20.33-20.48
3.66-3.69	2.56-2.59	6.34-6.39	15.09-15.19	25.99-26.24	6.59-6.63	10.25-10.32	20.49-20.64
3.70-3.73	2.60-2.63	6.40-6.45	15.20-15.30	26.25-26.50	6.65-6.68	10.33-10.40	20.65-20.80
3.74-3.77	2.64-2.67	6.46-6.51	15.31-15.42	26.51-26.76	6.69-6.73	10.41-10.48	20.81-20.96
3.78-3.81	2.68-2.71	6.52-6.57	15.43-15.54	26.77-27.02	6.74-6.78	10.49-10.56	20.97-21.12
3.82-3.85	2.72-2.75	6.58-6.63	15.55-15.66	27.03-27.28	6.79-6.83	10.57-10.64	21.13-21.28
3.86-3.89	2.76-2.79	6.64-6.68	15.67-15.79	27.29-27.54	6.84-6.88	10.65-10.72	21.29-21.44
3.90-3.93	2.80-2.83	6.70-6.75	15.80-15.92	27.55-27.80	6.89-6.93	10.73-10.80	21.45-21.61
3.94-3.98	2.84-2.88	6.76-6.81	15.93-16.06	27.81-28.06	6.94-7.00	10.81-10.90	21.62-21.88
3.99-4.03	2.89-2.93	6.82-6.87	16.07-16.20	28.07-28.31	7.01-7.06	10.91-11.00	21.89-22.09
4.04-4.08	2.94-2.98	6.88-6.93	16.21-16.35	28.32-28.55	7.07-7.12	11.01-11.09	22.10-22.30
4.09-4.13	2.99-3.03	6.94-6.99	16.36-16.51	28.56-28.80	7.13-7.18	11.10-11.19	22.31-22.50
4.14-4.18	3.04-3.08	7.00-7.05	16.52-16.68	28.81-29.06	7.19-7.25	11.20-11.29	22.51-22.72
4.19-4.24	3.09-3.14	7.06-7.12	16.69-16.86	29.07-29.34	7.26-7.32	11.30-11.40	22.73-22.95
4.25-4.30	3.15-3.20	7.13-7.19	16.87-17.05	29.35-29.63	7.33-7.39	11.41-11.51	22.96-23.19
4.31-4.36	3.21-3.26	7.20-7.26	17.06-17.25	29.64-29.91	7.40-7.46	11.52-11.62	23.20-23.43
4.37-4.42	3.27-3.32	7.27-7.33	17.26-17.46	29.92-30.19	7.47-7.53	11.63-11.73	23.44-23.69
4.43-4.48	3.33-3.38	7.34-7.40	17.47-17.67	30.20-30.50	7.54-7.61	11.74-11.85	23.70-23.95
4.49-4.54	3.39-3.44	7.41-7.50	17.68-17.88	30.51-30.91	7.62-7.71	11.86-12.01	23.96-24.27
4.55-4.60	3.45-3.50	7.51-7.60	17.89-18.09	30.92-31.32	7.72-7.81	12.02-12.17	24.28-24.64
4.61-4.70	3.51-3.60	7.61-7.70	18.10-18.30	31.33-31.74	7.82-7.91	12.18-12.33	24.65-24.98
4.71-4.80	3.61-3.70	7.71-7.80	18.31-18.55	31.75-32.15	7.92-8.02	12.34-12.49	24.99-25.30
4.81-4.90	3.71-3.80	7.81-7.90	18.56-18.81	32.16-32.56	8.03-8.12	12.50-12.65	25.31-25.65
4.91-5.00	3.81-3.90	7.91-8.00	18.82-19.12	32.57-33.06	8.13-8.25	12.66-12.85	25.65-25.99
5.0-5.1	3.9-4.0	8.0-8.1	19.2-19.6	33.1-33.7	8.3-8.4	12.9-13.1	26.0-26.5
5.1-5.2	4.0-4.1	8.1-8.2	19.6-20.0	33.7-34.3	8.4-8.5	13.1-13.3	26.5-27.0
5.2-5.3	4.1-4.2	8.2-8.3	20.0-20.4	34.3-35.0	8.5-8.7	13.3-13.6	27.0-27.5
5.3-5.5	4.2-4.4	8.3-8.5	20.4-20.8	35.0-35.6	8.7-8.9	13.6-13.9	27.5-28.0

*Timed from first foot contact over start line.
Possible inconsistency where there are specialist 60m indoor athletes.

Table 2: Bounding controls

*From standing.

Target Time	Standing Jump Long (m)	Reach (cm)	3 Bounds* (m)	5 Bounds* (m)	10 Bounds* (m)
10.20-10.65	2.90-3.20	76-85	9.20-10.00	15.90-17.10	29.50-39.50
10.70-11.10	2.70-3.00	68-88	8.50-9.10	14.60-15.60	27.00-37.00
11.20-11.70	2.60-2.90	60-69	7.90-8.50	14.00-15.00	25.00-35.00
11.80-12.20	2.50-2.80	53-61	7.50-8.10	13.40-14.40	23.00-33.00
12.30-12.70	2.40-2.70	46-54	7.20-7.80	12.80-13.80	21.00-31.00
12.80-13.20	2.30-2.60	39-47	6.80-7.40	12.20-13.20	19.00-29.00

Broad ranges reflect leg length variations as much as strength differences within groups. Coaches will establish tighter ranges for individual athletes and "height groups". **Note:** The data here represents a loose guide linking control and competition performance. Athletes may produce a given performance in competition *without* meeting all control criteria! Tables must be adapted and interpreted by coach and athlete accordingly.

The controls listed are by no means exhaustive. They should be adapted, added to, or rejected in light of establishing a relevant personal test battery.

1) Core Preparation Phase
  =6 weeks: November-Mid December
  =6-8 week: March-Mid/Late April

SPECIFIC STRENGTH (3 units per weekly microcycle)

OBJECTIVE: Sprint Drive
EXERCISE:

- Heavy harness sprints from crouch over 30m-40m x 3-4
- Left leg lead 10 bounds plus run out to 50m x 2-3
- Right leg lead to bounds plus run out to 50m x 2-3

OBJECTIVE: Sprint Stride
EXERCISE:

- Power running over 100m x 3-4
- Light harness from rolling start—fast over 30m x 3-4
- Alternate leg split tuck jumps—sets of 12 repetitions x 3-6
- High knee prancing over 40m-60m x 4-6
- Loaded thigh—high/fast knee lift max. possible speed of limb movement over 20-30m x 3-5

TRACK UNITS (3 units per 2 week microcycle)

OBJECTIVE: Technique Differentiation
EXERCISE:

- 3 x 2 x 150m 30m drive, 30m stride
- 30m lift, 30m stride, 30m lift
- 3 x 3 x 90m 30m drive, 30m stride 30m lift
- 3 x 3 x 90m (from roll), 30m stride 30m ease, 30m stride
- 3 x 4 x 50m—$3/4$—full speed—varying pace in mock race situations

The balance of training units are general strength units mixing body weight exercises with weight training; and track units such as 3 x 3 x 150m; 3 x 2 x 200m; 2 x 2 x 250m; or 2 x 2 x 300m to develop basic sprint stride, technique endurance.

2) Specific Preparation Phase
  =4 weeks: Mid-December—Mid-January
  =6-8 weeks: Mid/Late April-Mid-June

SPECIFIC STRENGTH (3 units per weekly microcycle)

As for the Core Preparation Phase

OBJECTIVE: Technique Differentiation Technique at progressive speed
EXERCISE:

- 3 x 2 x 30 drive, 30m stride, 30m lift
- 3 x 3 x 60m $3/4$—full speed
- 8 x 100m build-ups
- 3 x 3 x rolling 20m-30m

The balance of training units are high quality track units over 4 x 150m; 3 x 250m; 2 x 300m; build-ups over 6 x 200m; technique block work at $1/2$-$3/4$ speed—3 x 4 x 40m and one general strength unit per weekly microcycle. Regeneration units are not introduced.

3) Pre-Competition Phase

- 3 weeks mid-January—early February

(Special amps—preferably warm at altitude)—3-4 weeks mid June-early/mid July

SPECIFIC STRENGTH (1-2 units per weekly microcycle)

As for the core preparation phase

TRACK UNITS: Progression of maximum speed
EXERCISE:

- 3 x 3 x rolling 20m-30m
- 3 x 60m time trials
- 3 x 2 rolling 50m
- Training intensity competitions and relays

The balance of training units are time trials over 100m, 150m, 200m, 250m, 5 x 30m.

Training competitions from blocks, 6 x 100m, build-ups, 3 x 3 x 60m, $3/4$ speed, and regeneration units.

4) Competition Phase
  =4 weeks: Early February—Early March
  =8 weeks: Early/Mid July—Early September

WEEKLY MICROCYCLE

1. 2 x 3 x 120m quality speed relay
2. 3 x 2 x rolling maximum speed 30m
3. 3 x 50m competition runs in training
4. 3-5 x build-up 100m
5. 5 x 30m competition runs in training
6. Rest or high quality specific strength; or fast

47

light weights
7. Competition

IT IS A CONTEST—NOT A TIME TRIAL

Of course, the foregoing must be viewed against a background of a progression of balanced overall strength; technique drills; and sound medical and lifestyle management; all woven into a program over times ranging from 1-4 years.

In addition to a systematic approach to the physical preparation of the athlete for maximum speed—there must be meticulous preparation for the athlete for a variety of competition situations. While the word "concentration" is readily understood when it comes to expressing the lifing technique at maximum speed the focus of such concentration may not be when race situation variables are introduced. The thought processes in chasing and catching an opponent are not the same as those when running at an opponent; nor when chasing but failing to catch an opponent.

The coach must ensure that the athlete has opportunity to learn appropriate thought processes through the experience of the full range of race situations.

More than this, there must be regular return to such learning situations under increasing pressure so the athlete's performance capacity improves.

CONCLUSION

The sprinter's development of maximum speed—both in terms of time for 100m and speed achieved within the run—rests squarely on establishing a sound technical model, improving relevant physical ability, then building towards expressing the technical model at progressive speed through those stimuli which facilitate speed both in training and competition. The key technique is the sprint stride—with the sprint lift (maximum speed) and sprint drive (start and acceleration) built onto this technique. While stride, lift and drive are each practiced separately, they are consequently referred to the continuous whole of the linked sections of the discipline. In the final analysis, the discipline is, however, a contest and athletes must learn through competition and experience to master the range of situations which head to head 100m competition implies.

VIEWS ON SPRINT TRAINING

by Boris Tabatshnik, USSR

The author, who coaches the Soviet Union's national experimental sprint squad, outlines sample training programs for the 17 to 20 years age range and presents summaries of the changes in the emphasis of different training means that occur within a training year, as well as from one year to the next.

The author recommends that the training of sprinters must be well balanced and the development of speed should take place all year round with the exception of the transition period.

As can be seen in the summary of the suggested sample training programs (Table 3), the largest maximal speed development volumes occur in December-January and April-May. The largest volume of strength exercises takes place in March-April, while jumping and bounding exercise have the highest volumes in October-November and again in April-May.

The volume of intensive repetition runs over distances exceeding 80m reaches the highest volumes in December-January and April-May. The aerobic-anaerobic repetition runs have the highest volume in October-November, the aerobic repetition runs in October-November and March-April.

The sample training schedules, presented below, are based on a double periodized year, aiming to produce the first peak during the winter indoor competitions and the second peak during the outdoor season.

GENERAL PREPARATION PERIOD

Day 1:
Easy jogging over 800 to 1000m, general exercises, sprinting drills (300 to 400m), bounding over 10 hurdles from double-legged takeoffs (8 to 10 reps), shot throws (10 to 15 reps). Two acceleration runs over 60 to 80m, varied speed runs (6 to 8 reps) over 100m (40m fast + 30m relaxed + 30m fast). Stretching exercises.

Day 2:
Easy jogging over 100m, medicine ball exercises (50 to 70 throws), acceleration runs over 60m (3 reps).

10 to 15 practice starts, high knee lift runs over 100m (5 to 6 reps), bounding, 800m of slow running.

Day 3:
Warm-up. Weight training—clean and jerk: 6 to 8 reps. 50kg, 3 to 4 reps. 60kg, 1 to 2 reps. 70kg, 1 rep. 75kg, 1 reps 80kg. Snatch: 3 sets of 6 to 8 reps. 40 to 50kg. Squat: 8 to 10 reps. 80kg. 5 to 8 reps. 90kg, 2 to 3 reps. 100kg, 1 to 2 reps. 110kg, 1 rep. 125kg. Bounding over 10 hurdles, stretching exercises.

Day 4:
Slow running 10 to 15 minutes, general exercises, running and bounding uphill (3 to 5° incline) over 60m (6 to 8 reps) and 150 to 200m (6 reps). 10 minutes of slow running.

Day 5:
Slow running over 1200 to 1500m, general exercises, 8 to 10 reps of 10—jumps, upstairs jumps (4 to 8 reps). Repetition runs (80 to 90% intensity) over 300 + 250 + 200 + 150m with walk back recoveries over the same distance.

Day 6:
Weight training—bench press (percent of body weight): 3 sets of 3 to 5 reps (80 to 100%), 3 sets of 5 to 7 reps (100 to 120%), 3 sets of 10 to 15 reps (80%). Bounding in half knee bend position: 3 sets of 10 to 15 reps (100 to 120%). 20 minutes of easy cross country running, stretching exercises.

Day 7:
Rest.

SPECIFIC PREPARATION PERIOD

Day 1:
Easy jogging, general exercises, shot throws

forward-upward (10 reps). 3 reps of 60m accelerations, 10 to 15 practice starts, 2 reps of 100m accelerations + 2 reps of 100m acceleration with a 3kg weight vest, 2 reps of 100m (90 to 95% intensity). Recoveries between repetitions 3 to 4 minutes between series 5 to 7 minutes. Stretching exercises, slow running.

Day 2:
Easy jogging, general exercises, sprinting drills (5 reps of 30m), standing long jumps (10 reps), standing triple jumps (5 reps). 60m sprints with a weight vest (5 to 6 reps), 150m runs (2 to 3 reps). Recoveries 5 to 6 minutes. Stretching exercises.

Day 3:
Slow running (10 minutes), weight training—clean and jerk: 3 to 4 reps. 60kg, 1 to 2 reps. 70kg, 1 rep. 75 to 80kg, 1 rep. 80 to 90kg. Snatch: 3 to 5 reps. 50kg, 1 to 2 reps. 60kg. Half-squat: 6 reps. 80kg, 6 to 8 reps. 100kg, 5 to 7 reps. 110kg, 3 to 5 reps. 120kg, 2 to 3 reps. 130kg (stretching exercises between the lifts). Bounding over 10 hurdles (10 reps), easy accelerations over 60 to 80m (3 reps), jogging.

Day 4:
10 to 12 minutes easy running, general exercises, bounding and sprinting drills. 200m repetition runs with the first 120 to 150m uphill (3 to 4°) with 90% intensity (4 to 5 reps). Recoveries 7 to 8 minutes.

Day 5:
Slow running over 1200 to 1500m, general exercises, sprinting drills. Two 80m accelerations at maximal intensity, followed by 80m repetitions (4 to 5) with 5 to 6 minute recoveries. 90% intensity runs 250 + 200 + 150m with 8 to 10 minute recoveries.

Day 6:
Easy warm-up, general exercises, bounding over 80 to 100m (3 reps intensive, 3 reps relaxed), stretching exercises.

Day 7:
Rest.

TRAINING DURING INDOOR SEASON

Day 1:
Warm-up, shot throws (10 reps), standing long jump (10 reps), standing triple jump (5 reps). Accelerations over 60m (4 reps), 6 to 8 crouch starts over 20 to 30m, 150m runs with 90 to 95% intensity (3 to 4 reps). Recoveries 8 to 10 minutes. Slow running for 10 minutes.

Day 2:
Slow running, general exercises, sprinting drills over 30m (4 to 6 reps), 3 crouch starts over 20m, 5 over 30m, 5 x 30m from flying start, stretching exercises.

Day 3:
Slow running, general exercises, sprinting drills over 30 to 40m (5 reps), repetitions runs 250 + 200 + 150m with 95% intensity. Recoveries 8 to 10 minutes. Slow running.

Day 4:
Rest.

Day 5:
Warm-up, very fast sprinting drills, 2 crouch starts over 30m, 3 over 40m. Relay changeovers at full speed. Easy running for 10 minutes, stretching exercises.

Day 6:
Warm-up, shot throws (10 reps). Timed accelerations over 60m (3 reps) and 30m (5 to 7 reps), relaxed 80 to 100m repetitions (5 to 6 reps) with 5 to 7 minute recoveries.

Day 7:
Rest.

Friday's training is very light in case there is a competition on Saturday. Restoration measures include easy cross country running, massage and sauna.

PRE SEASON TRAINING (SPRING)

Day 1:
Warm-up, sprinting drills over 40 to 50m (5 to 6 reps), standing long jump (10 reps), standing triple jump (5 reps), 10 jumps (5 reps). 6 to 8 crouch starts over 20 to 30m, repetition runs over 100m (4 to 5 reps), shot throws (10 to 15 reps). 800m of slow running.

Day 2:
Slow running over 800 to 1000m, general exercises, sprinting drills over 50 to 60m (5 reps), 3 accelerations of 60 to 80m. Starting practice—3 x 30m, 1 x 40m, 1 x 50m, 1 x 60m. Relay changeovers. 800m of easy running.

Day 3:
Warm-up, general exercises, hurdling drills, repetition runs over 150m (3 reps) with 95 to 98% intensity. Relaxation exercises.

Day 4:
Active rest.

Day 5:
15 to 20 minutes of easy running, accelerations over 80m (2 to 4 reps), 2 x 20m + 2 x 30m + 2 x 60m from crouch start. Full speed relay changeovers, easy running, stretching exercises.

Day 6:
Warm-up, shot throws (10 to 15 reps), strength development exercises. Varied speed runs over 100m (5 to 6 reps) with 100m jog recoveries.

Day 7:
Rest.

COMPETITION PERIOD

Day 1:
Warm-up (30 to 40 minutes), shot throws (8 to 10 reps), sprinting drills. Acceleration runs over 80m (3 reps) and 120m (4 reps), stretching exercises.

Day 2:
Easy running over 800m. General exercises (20 minutes), 2 to 3 accelerations over 60 to 100m, crouch starts (3 x 30m, 2 x 60m, 2 x 80m). Jogging.

Day 3:
Warm-up, standing long jumps (8 to 10 reps), standing triple jumps (5 reps), standing 5-jumps (5 reps). Weight training with light weights, employing 5 or 6 exercises to improve muscle tone. Easy sprints on the grass over 80 to 100m (4 to 5 reps). Stretching exercises.

Day 4:
Rest.

Day 5:
Easy running, 15 to 20 minutes general exercises, a few sprinting drills, 2 acceleration runs, 4 to 5 starts over 30m, relaxation exercises.

Day 6:
Competition.

Day 7:
Competition.

Regular tests to evaluate progress are most helpful during the competition period. The suggested standards for the young sprinters in the 17 to 20 years age range are presented in Table 1. The changes in the loads of training means are presented for the same age range in Table 2.

Table 1: Control standards for young sprinters in the competition period.

Test	Standards	
	Men	Women
60m crouch start (sec.)	6.7-6.6	7.5-7.4
100m crouch start (sec.)	10.7-10.5	11.8-11.7
200m crouch start (sec.)	21.6-21.2	24.5-24.0
30m crouch start (sec.)	3.8-3.7	4.3-4.2
30m flying start (sec.)	2.8-2.7	3.3-3.2
150m (sec.)	16.0-15.8	17.8-17.5
300m (sec.)	35.0-34.5	41.0-40.0
Standing long jump (m)	2.95-3.05	2.65-2.75
Standing triple jump (m)	8.90-9.50	7.50-8.00
Standing 10-jump (m)	33.00-34.50	28.50-29.50

Table 2: Changes in the basic training means for sprinters in the 17 to 20 year age range (total for a year).

	Training means	17-18 yrs.	18-19 yrs.	19-20 yrs.
Volume in km	Up to 80m distances (100-90%) Anaerobic-alactic	20	22	25
	Over 80m distance (100-71%) Anaerobic-glycolytic	25	35	40
	Over 80m distances (90-81%) Aerobic-anaerobic	30	25	20
	Over 80m distances (80% or less) Aerobic	55	50	45
	Number of starts in training	1100	1200	1300
	Number of jumping exercises (take-offs)	10,000	10,000	10,000
	Number of competitions	40	45	50

Finally, a summary that shows the changes in the various means during a training year, indicating the months during which the highest and lowest volumes of a particular developmental aspect occurs.

Table 3: The changes of emphasis on training means during a training year.

	Training means	Oct-Nov	Dec-Jan	Jan-Feb	March-Apr	Apr-May	May-June	July-Aug
Volume in km	Up to 80m (100-96%)	1.5	4	3	1	4.5	3	3
	Over 80m (100-91%)	2	8	3	3	3	3	3
	Over 80m (90-81%)	10	2	1	8	3	1	3
	Over 80m (80% and less)	15	4	2	15	5	2	2
	Number of starts	100	200	150	100	200	150	200
	Take-offs in jumps	2500	800	500	500	2500	500	700
	Weight lifts in tons	50	20	8	40	15	10	10

TRAINING PROCEDURES IN SPRINTING

by Valeriy Borzov, USSR

Munich Olympics double gold medalist Valeriy Borzov discusses the principles employed by his coach, Valentin Petrovski, in sprint training. The article is based on translated extracts from Borzov's recent book, titled "10 Seconds—A Lifetime"

Valentin Petrovski, who coached me, believed that the first task before the start of the season—faced by the coach and the athlete—is to decide how to reach in eight or nine months time at a fixed date of a major competition a performance that exceeds previous season's results. Naturally, something had to be changed in the condition of the athlete, otherwise there would be no improvement. However, what has to be changed and how much?

A simple solution in this situation is to increase the load in all training phases, hoping that the improved level of performance capacities will automatically assure better results. This approach can be dangerous. Results in sprinting (also in other events) do not depend on one performance factor only, for example, speed, but a variety of factors: speed, speed endurance, power, etc. Further complications are added by the possibility that an over-development of one factor can often be responsible for a drop in another performance area. For example, an improvement in speed endurance can take place at the cost of a drop in pure speed. Consequently, all performance factors have to be developed in an optimal relationship to each other.

Petrovski was a biologist and looked upon all changes in the training process as corresponding functional changes in the organism. This meant that in order to achieve better performances all the sub-systems of the organism—neuromuscular, cardiovascular, ventilation, etc.—had to be developed to reach new, correctly planned levels.

Petrovski, after evaluating my 1968 preparations, compared this information with the world's best sprinters. It revealed that, while I had recorded 10.2 seconds for the 100m, my maximum speed and acceleration ability were below the world's best. The comparison made my task clear, I had to improve my start, the acceleration phase and lift the maximum speed level. What was left to

decide was to clarify to what level these parameters had to be improved in the training process and what changes had to occur in the performance indicators.

The following indicators were selected for the evaluation: 30m from a flying start to evaluate maximum speed, 30m and 60m from a crouch start to evaluate the efficiency of the start and the rate of acceleration. The times of 100m and 200m were used to evaluate speed endurance. Assuming that sprint times depend mainly on the start, the acceleration, maximum speed and speed endurance, all that was left was to decide how these indicators had to correlate with concrete 100 and 200m times.

Petrovski had for this task established a table of evaluation indicators, based on the performances recorded by Soviet, as well as foreign sprinters. The table, slightly changed according to practical experience, still serves a useful purpose today. (see Table 1).

Table 1

Speed (m/sec)	Flying 30m	Crouch start			
		30m	60m	100m	200m
12.0	2.5	3.5	6.4	9.9	20.2
11.5	2.6	3.6	6.5	10.1	20.6
11.1	2.7	3.7	6.6	10.3	21.0
10.7	2.8	3.8	6.8	10.6	21.6
10.3	2.9	3.9	6.9	10.8	22.0
10.0	3.0	4.0	7.0	11.0	22.4

I will use some examples to show how to use Petrovski's table. Let us assume that I clocked 3.5 seconds in the 30m test from a crouch start and 6.5 seconds in the 60m from a crouch start. At the same time my competitive 100m performance was 10.4 seconds. These results, as my 30m time from a flying start was equivalent to 11.5m/seconds, indicated that I lacked speed endurance. However, if for example, I would have clocked 10.2 seconds in a 100m race but only 6.8 seconds for the 60m crouch start test, the results would show a poor acceleration phase but excellent speed endurance.

In 1968 my performance indicators were as follows: 30m from a flying start—2.7 seconds, 30m from a crouch start—3.7 seconds and 60m from a crouch start—6.6 seconds. Petrovski had planned for me to reach 10.0 seconds in the following year to compete successfully in the European Championships. This meant that I had to reach in my preparation the following indicators: 30m from a flying start—2.6 seconds, 30m from a crouch start—3.6 seconds, 60m from a crouch start—6.5 seconds. We concentrated on the 100m because there wasn't sufficient time to lift speed endurance to a level required to contest successfully the 200m event.

As it can be seen, I had to improve all my performance indicators by a margin of 0.1 seconds. This meant a full year of well planned work besides finding ways and means to employ the most efficient training methods. We had to discover an approach to training that would make it possible to break the so-called "speed barriers" and Petrovski found the answer.

Petrovski's search for an answer was based on the understanding that a certain performance in the 100m requires a corresponding level of maximum speed and speed endurance. By maximum speed we mean the fastest a sprinter is capable of over a short section of the whole distance. Speed endurance is the capacity to maintain a certain speed in a time unit or over a distance. Naturally, different 100m performances require different levels of maximum speed and speed endurance.

The lifting of required capacities to certain levels can be achieved by using different types of repetitions over 30 to 400m distances. However, it is known that the effectiveness of training depends not only on the choice of methods used, but also how these methods are employed. Let us assume that I am working on the development of speed. After the warm-up, I will run the first repetition over 60m. How long should it be before I start the second repetition? What should be the recovery time that would produce best dividends for the development of maximum speed?

Scientific research has indicated that fatigue after any type of workload brings about several changes in the work capacity of the organism. It has been established that there are four recovery stages in this situation and the improvement, or otherwise, of the functional capacities of the organism depends

Valeriy Borzov

in which recovery stage the new workload is introduced. Petrovski used this information to establish three different combinations of load and recovery relationship—methods A, B and C.

In **method A** each repetition is performed in the first recovery stage, i.e., after a short time unit when the organism is still in the low phase of work capacity. This method is used to develop speed endurance. The maximum speed level remains unchanged or in some cases (when this method is used for a long time) even drops.

In using **method B** each repetition is performed in the second recovery stage when endurance, compared with the initial level, is lower but muscular power, speed and movement coordination are at a higher level. This method brings about an efficient development of maximum speed. Speed endurance remains unchanged or improves a little.

In **method C** each repetition is performed in the third recovery phase when work capacity indicators have reached their initial level. This method has a limited training effect but can be used to maintain form. It has little influence on the development of maximum speed and none on the development of endurance.

The methods established by Petrovski made it possible for us to find an optimal approach to training and adjust the work in any required direction. Consequently, if my performance indicators showed the need to develop maximum speed, I adopted method B and covered 60m repetitions with a minute or minute and a half recoveries. When the aim was to develop speed endurance the recoveries were reduced to 45 seconds.

I would like to give credit to Petrovski, who understood my condition in each training phase, realizing when to increase training loads and when to employ tapering in order to recover before the introduction of the next load. His excellent intuition was, of course, based on his wide knowledge in biology, psychology and physiology, reflected in a precise tuning of my body for important competitions.

My last two weeks prior to competitions were always carefully planned. The training load was exactly established and the recovery organized, using massage, vitamin intake and active rest. I faced competitions with improved performance capacity and mentally rested, in other words—completely prepared for the race. It should be added that Petrovski never set "win or die" tasks. Instead, when he believed that I was ready for a 10.4 seconds 100m clocking, the task was to reach a time in the 10.4 to 10.5 region. This protected me from negative emotions (there was nothing lost if I failed to win, provided my performance was closest to the estimated time) and reinforced my belief in the skills and foresight of the coach.

DEVELOPING MAXIMUM RUNNING SPEED

by Brent McFarlane, Canada

Canadian National Coach, Brent McFarlane, looks into the development of maximum sprinting speed by pinpointing the physiological and biomechanical background of the task before presenting suggestions on the methods and innovative ideas to achieve the objective.

One of the major problems facing us in reading, interpreting and using various forms and studies on the development of maximum speed is the lack of common and accurate terminology. Scientists often disagree on many areas—what are we, as coaches, to do? Before I continue, let me clearly state that I am a working coach, who applies scientific information I understand to a given environment and the individual athletes within that framework. To bridge the gap between science and coaching can sometimes leave one frustrated. I simply wish to leave you with some "food for thought" on how to develop maximum running speed. In this regard it is essential to:

- pinpoint the fundamentals and offer accurate and working definitions of terms
- ensure that sufficient consideration is given to the biomechanics, physiology and specificity of the development of maximum speed
- present hints on teaching methods and innnovative ideas to meet the above objectives.

Differences in the interpretation of the "correct" methods to develop maximum speed have led to a variety of successful systems. As a coach, and not a scientist, you must be able to interpret, adjust and apply current scientific information to suit your given situation and athletes. Keeping in mind that all programs must first be designed to prevent injuries, a coach can then develop a system based on:

- the age and number of years an athlete has been involved in sport
- the athlete's individual strengths and weaknesses, based on a battery of tests (30m run, jumps decathlon, body measurements, etc.)
- an event specific program based on specialization, in this case sprinting speed.

SPEED

A Definition

"Sprinters are born, not made" is an axiom of many coaches. Does this really apply? Let's consider a few facts about physiology in terms of energy systems. The anaerobic (without oxygen) alactic (without lactate) energy system, more commonly referred to as "SPEED", is best challenged as an athlete approaches top speed between 30 and 60m while running at 95% to 100% of maximum. This high intensity work occurs without the build-up of significant lactate (lactic acid, hydrogen ions and other wastes). This speed component of anaerobic metabolism lasts for approximately six seconds and should be trained when no muscle fatigue is present (usually after 24 to 36 hours of rest or very low intensity work). Therefore, speed can be defined as runs at 95% to 100% over 30 to 60m, or six seconds of running at maximum effort.

Background

Sprinting is learned through motor educability. The technique of sprinting must be rehearsed at slow speeds and then transferred to runs at maximum speed. Athletes may run only as fast as their technique allows. Sprinting involves moving the body's limbs at the highest possible velocity. The stimulation, excitation and correct firing order of the motor units makes it possible for high frequency movements to occur. The whole process is not totally clear but the complex coordination and timing of the motor units and muscles most certainly must be rehearsed at high speeds to implant the correct patterns.

Speed is limited by the athlete's technique. An athlete cannot run faster than his technique will allow. There is no room for error. Repetition of mistakes means perfection of errors.

Speed = stride frequency x stride length.

Stride frequency is directly related to the number of fast and slow twitch fibers found in the muscle. More specifically, it involves the selective recruitment of motor unit pathways to improve the firing of the correct motor units to give the greatest rate of force. Sprinters with more fast twitch fibers (primarily in the flexors) have a higher threshold for firing, which do not fire under moderate work loads. Speed seems to be more related to synchronizing and firing the correct motor units, rather than the high lactate environment using different energy systems.

Stride length can be improved by developing muscular strength, power, strength endurance and proper running technique. Impulse = force x time. In the initial acceleration phase for sprinting there is a relatively long period of time to develop and apply force to create a maximum impulse. The angular velocity of the lower leg is relatively slow and, as speed increases, the time, force and impulse decrease . . . and the angular velocity increases. Flexibility and a correct warm up will affect stride length and frequency.

It is easy to see that developments in speed are highly specific. To summarize: (1) Speed training must be performed by using brief intervals with high angular velocity. This will ultimately bring into play the correct neuromuscular pathways and energy sources used. (2) Skill development (technique) must be pre-learned, rehearsed and perfected before it can be done at brief interval high speed levels. (3) Flexibility must be developed, maintained and developed year round. (4) Strength developments must be parallel with developments in speed.

TECHNIQUE

First Derivatives

In many European countries today, skill or technique development for speed involves drills of extremely rapid movements with a series of sensations where the legs are in exact symmetry. Athletes rehearse every conceivable sensation at high velocity. Drills designed to focus on the exact components of high velocity running are known as first derivatives.

While experimenting with different levels of intensity at high speeds athletes learn to relax, change gear and perfect technique. Remember, any change in technique is a change that will affect speed. It has been my observation of Eastern European athletes that first derivatives are done best when the recovery foot is pulled through above the driving knee. A loose quad will allow

this to happen which will ultimately increase the angular velocity of the whole lower leg. It is also obvious that runs at top speed "come through the ankles". Simply, how fast can you move your feet and ankles?

Examples of first derivatives are:

- runs downhill or with the wind at high velocity
- many European countries have indoor training areas which have movable surfaces which can be elevated to a 3 to 5% incline to allow athletes to run virtually downhill at whatever angle they wish
- the USSR has a computerized pully system which pulls athletes at whatever speed they choose.

Second Derivatives

Basically, sprinting involves falling forward and recovering. To develop the correct stride length and maximize the frequency requires a series of basic drills which can isolate and combine a joint(s) to the specificity of sprinting at high velocity. These basic, or general drills are called second derivatives.

Sprinting involves learning through kinesthesis—teaching the body to feel certain sensations. The learning and perfection of technique must be done correctly. Performing technique incorrectly means the perfection of errors. Therefore, STOP, if this happens. To make corrections of poor technique may take months or even years.

To begin with, examine carefully the diagrams of the A and B exercises in Figure 1. They involve three action forms—walking (marching), skipping and running (sprinting).

A's march, skip, sprint (1 or 2 legs)

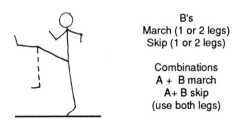

B's
March (1 or 2 legs)
Skip (1 or 2 legs)

Combinations
A + B march
A + B skip
(use both legs)

Figure 1: The A and B exercise drills.

A's, or high knee lift drills, begin with one leg. Stress the actions of a high knee lift, hips tall, cocked ankle, arm alignment in front of the body, active ankle landing and staying stretched tall. The arm action should be a punching action from the hip to shoulder height. Once one leg has been perfected, do the other leg and then alternate legs. After the basic walking (marching) drills progress to skipping and then running on the spot. A coach may choose to walk slowly beside athletes while they perform these drills to encourage, instruct and evaluate technique. B's, or leg extensions, follow the same learning sequence. Avoid B's in the running form. Combinations of A's and B's can be one with each leg doing an A or B exercise.

Remember, athletes can only run as fast as their technique allows. If two athletes are equal, the one who makes the least mistakes will come out ahead. In addition, poor technique will lead to poor body position, slower turnover, overstriding, collapsed hips, braking and tension. An athlete is as strong as his weakest link.

STRENGTH

One of the problems facing us in interpreting and using various forms of strength training is the lack of common and accurate terminology. Strength gains result from using a resistance. Three types of strength need to be defined more specifically:

Gross or maximum strength is closely related to isometric contractions, as it involves optimal muscle tension at very low velocity. It is best developed by loading between 90% (sub-max) and 100% (max) doing a small number of reps (1-5) and 3-5 sets with a varied recovery of 2-5 minutes.

Power (explosive, fast, elastic) strength is the maximum force a muscle can exert over a short period of time (less than 10 seconds or less than 10 reps), while producing muscle force under conditions of speed. It is best developed by loading between 75% and 90% maximum, doing 6-8 (10) reps with 3-4 sets and 1-3 minute recovery.

Strength endurance is the ability of a muscle to maintain its contractile force over a period of time (more than 10 seconds or more than 10 reps). It is best developed by loading between 50% to 75% of maximum , doing 12-24 (or more) reps with 3-4 sets and varied recovery of 45 to 90 seconds.

Basically, strength gains result from using a resistance in one of the following methods:

- using the body weight as a resistance (circuit or stage training, using basic exercises such as pushups, situps, squats, chinups)
- using the falling body weight as a resistance (depth jumping, hurdle hops, bounding)
- using weight as a resistance (free weights exercise machines)
- using weighted objects while simulating specific skills (weight vest, weighted shoes, sandbags, medicine balls)
- mechanical devices used as a resistance to specific movements (cables, accelerator, harness, computerized pully).

All strength programs should first be designed to prevent injuries and then develop strength and speed. Obviously, increases in strength will ultimately assist in a longer stride, more ankle drive, a stronger pillar (abdomen and back) to absorb force, and less chance of injuries. Without getting into the complexities of strength training and its endless ramifications, I would like to make a few basic suggestions with regard to developing speed in line with strength.

Pillar: The area of the abdomen and back should be one of the major concerns in the development of speed. All forces go through this area and, if it is not strong, technical problems will immediately become evident. Running tall requires the pillar to support the upper body in a way that the attachments (arms and legs) can work together without rotations, collapsing, overstriding, hips dropping and non-active foot placement. Our training cycles involve thousands of abdomen and back exercises using strength endurance (i.e., 5000 situps in one session).

Ankle: Runs at top speed go through the ankles. The ankle is a major area for strength concern. Injuries to the achilles, calf, feet and ankle joint itself can put an athlete out for a season. By using strength endurance and exercises such as ankle hops, toe raises at different angles, walking on toes, toe in, toe out walks, cable work and eventually work over hurdles (hops, jumps), depth jumping and bounding. . . many potential problem areas are eliminated.

Running knee lifts: are universally accepted throughout the world as a method to develop technique under power (speed) and strength endurance conditions. For power they are performed in the running form for 10 to 20m with anything over 20m being strength endurance. We have done up to 300m of running this way in one session. The technical and strength components of this drill canot be expressed enough in the development of speed variables.

Devices: Today, many new and creative devices have hit the market. John Mumford, Canada's national sprint coach, has developed an "Accelerator," a device which is attached to an athlete's waist and connected to a wheel with varying tensions. After runs of 30 to 100m, using the accelerator, the resistance is removed and improvements in stride frequency, technique, foot placement and running times are evident. Similar type work can done with a restraining belt or harness. Work with trampoline cables has a similar affect when used to do knee lift drills and then runs over 30 to 50m.

Weighted Objects: Runs using a weight vest, weight belt, weight shoes or sandbags are not new. Runs with and without these resistances seems to have a positive affect on speed development.

THE WARM-UP

To meet the needs of our training group we have four different warm-up series, each with a definite purpose and sequence. Too often warm-up procedures are non-structured, non-specific and lack in rehearsing the specifics of the event. A properly designed and sequenced warm-up prevents injuries and has a direct correlation with the results an athlete wishes to achieve at top speed.

Three laws of training apply to flexibility:
1. Specificity—exercises must focus on the joint(s) action and event demands.
2. Overloading—gains in flexibility occur when the limit of the existing range of movement is reached regularly, allowing new limits to be set.
3. Reversibility—improvements in flexibility will be lost if regular work is not maintained. An elite athlete may deteriorate after three days if some form of flexibility is not performed.

For simplicity, the warm-up used for a speed session will be broken into two parts:

PART I (20-30 minutes maximum)
This initial series of exercises involve "kinetic" flexibility (also called ballistic, bouncing, dynamic), using repeated movements through a range of motion at a joint(s) by applying momentum (swinging, bouncing, flexing actions).

All joints are worked gradually and easily. Kinesthesis combines the technical skills of sprinting with the correct neuromuscular patterns necessary to stimulate the complexities of the flexors and extensors associated with high velocity running. No static flexibility (holding, PNF) is done before maximum velocity runs. Basically, part 1 involves a 800 to 2000m jog followed by:

- 3 x 50m to 100m (easy jog)
- upper body kinetic flexibility (shoulder rotations, arm circle, hip circles)
- 3 x 50m to 100m (increase tempo of jog)
- lower body kinetic flexibility (ankle stretches, toe touching, bum kicks, knee lifts to front and side, swinging leg drills to front and side of the body, lots of leg shaking between exercises).

PART 2 (30 to 40 minutes in spikes).
This second part of the warm up is extremely specific to high velocity running (first derivative).

- 2 x 40m gradual acceleration with a walk back for recovery
- 2 x 50m as follows: falling start and gradual acceleration for 20m, followed by fast frequency, fast feet, short arm action for the next 30m
- 2 x 20m stressing fast frequency, fast feet, fast arms (no emphasis on stride length or tension of any form in runs)
- 2—3 x 60m as follows: falling start and gradual acceleration for 30m followed by 30m of fast frequency (fast feet and arms)
- good recovery between repetitions (5 to 8 minutes) and 20 minute break before racing.

To conclude, during major competitions athletes should warm up by themselves with no distractions. The rehearsal done in the warm up is critical in the total puzzle of developing maximum speed.

TRAINING

It is very questionable if speed training does affect the energy system involved—namely the anaerobic alactic. Again, as mentioned, speed seems to be more related to the recruitment and firing of fast twitch fibers. The secret to speed may lie in the central nervous system. However, the basic sequencing of loads and correct overloading methods on the body seem to have a very positive influence on speed development. The computer age has brought with it a more in depth scientific pool of knowledge to be used by the coach. For some time progressive loading tables have been used to produce maximum runs using speed. A sample for loading and sequencing speed is shown in Table 1.

It should be noted that fatigue should not be present when performing speed work. Sets of three to four repetitions with one to three minute recoveries between repetitions and 10 to 15 minutes between sets are recommended. No more than four sets, or 450 to 500m, should ever be included in a speed session.

Submaximal speed work (90 to 95%), involving slower turns and more emphasis on technique, can be performed over the same distance but remember that the recruitment and firing of motor units will not reach the same magnitude. The technical ability of an individual dictates the running speed. Components of speed are included in the training program year-round with the maximum intensity reached in the major competition phase.

Recovery is essential in maximizing the development of speed. Best results are usually achieved after 24 to 36 hours or rest. Recoveries may be in the form of rest or easy jogging, or a flexibility session. It may involve the use of an electrical stimulator, using hydrotherapy, or simple massage. Recovery weeks in the training program are also critical. Three mini-cycles (10 days) with built-in recovery days are used. Alternating hard and easy days provides adequate rest to athletes in speed related events. The day (or two) before a major event is usually set aside for recovery. Any fatigue present will affect results.

In conclusion, my acknowledgements and thanks to Charlie Francis (Canada), Brion McKinnon (Canada), Sandy Ewen (Scotland) and John Mumford (Canada).

Table 1: Workouts

Distance	1		2		3		4		5		6	
30	3x30	90	4x30	120	5x30	150	2(3x30)	180	2(4x30)	240	2(5x30)	300
40	3x40	120	4x40	160	5x40	200	2(3x40)	240	2(4x40)	320	2(5x40)	400
50	3x50	150	4x50	120	5x50	250	2(3x50)	300	2(4x50)	400	2(5x50)	500
60	3x60	180	4x60	160	5x60	300	2(3x60)	360	2(4x60)	480	-	
30 - 40	2x30 1x40	100	3x30 2x40	170	4x30 3x40	240	5x30 4x40	310	2(3x30) 2x40	200	2(4x30) 3x40	360
40 - 50	2x40 1x50	130	3x40 2x50	220	4x40 3x50	310	5x40 4x50	400	2(3x40) 2x50	340	2(4x40) 3x50	470
50 - 60	2x50 1x60	160	3x50 2x60	270	4x50 3x60	380	5x50 4x60	490	2(3x50) 2x60	420	-	
20 - 30 - 40	2x(20, 30, 40)	180	2x(20, 30) 3x40	220	2x20 3x(30, 40)	250	3x(20, 30, 40)	280	3x(20, 30) 4x40	310	3x20 4x(30, 40)	340
30 - 40 - 50	2x(30, 40, 50)	240	2x(30, 40) 3x50	290	2x30 3x(40, 50)	330	3x(30, 40, 50)	360	3x(30, 40) 4x50	410	3x30 4x(40, 50)	450
40 - 50 - 60	2x(40, 50, 60)	300	2x(40, 50) 3x60	360	2x40 3x(50, 60)	410	3x(40, 50, 60)	450	3x(40, 50) 4x50	470	-	

NOTE: Sets of 3 to 4 rep. with 1 to 3 min. between reps. and 10 to 15 min. between sets is recommended. No more than 4 sets or 450-500m total should ever be done in a speed session. The second column in each workout presents the total distance.

STARTING DRILLS FOR SPRINTERS

by Aleksandr Goldrin, USSR

The author presents a series of novel drills to improve and teach the sprint start. Some of the exercises are also valuable for the development of specific power.

Sprints contain two major phases—the acceleration to maximal speed and the maintenance of it. Both phases have to be developed in training. This text covers the first, the reaching of maximal speed. Factors, such as the development of physical capacities, the placement of starting blocks and the different crouch start positions, as well as a variety of exercises to learn and improve the start, are thoroughly covered in technical literature. However, this writer, continually looking for new and more efficient methods to improve the start, gradually developed some new drills.

The drills, described below, make it possible to reduce considerably the volume of power development exercises in order to reduce injury risks. They also have proved to be most effective, particularly in training periods prior to peak performances. Coaches and athletes can use the drills for variety, selecting the most suitable for a particular training phase according to the physical capacities of an athlete and the training tasks.

The description of the recommended drills that follow is not given in any particular order. They can be chosen and performed according to individual needs.

STARTING DRILLS

Exercise 1:

This drill requires the use of a treadmill that is about 100 to 120cm long and not over 40 to 50cm wide. The narrow width is helpful because it forces a straight feet placement in the acceleration.

The treadmill run that imitates the starting acceleration allows the development of rhythm and coordination. It is helpful in improving speed in the acceleration phase and gives the coach an excellent opportunity to make corrections while the athlete is running.

Exercise 2:

In the performance of this exercise the coach has to be equipped with roller skates. The exercise allows the polishing of starting technique while the athlete develops muscular strength specific to the starting procedures. The coach is in a position to control and correct movements while the athlete is in action.

Exercise 3:

A rope with a rotating cylinder, that can be regulated with a break, is needed. It is best to have the end of the rope attached to the athlete's shoulders, because the attachment to the hips can be responsible for an early lifting of the shoulders.

This exercise allows the improvement of single movement in the start, teaches the athlete to use strength in all the starting phases and develops power in all muscle groups involved. The athlete is in a good position to control his movements, adjusted to the individual needs by the break.

Exercise 4:

A rubber cord connects two runners in the normal crouch start position with the rear runner assisted in this position by the coach. The front runner is the first to begin after the command to start.

The main aim of this exercise is to develop the starting speed, to establish a firm competitive rhythm and to correct the common fault of jumping out from the blocks. It should be used only after the start is reasonably well established so that the athletes can concentrate on relaxation and maximal acceleration.

Exercise 5:

Two rubber cords are attached to the athlete's shoulders or hips with the other ends connected to posts or some other immobile objects. The length of the rubber cords and their tensity are adjusted to individual needs but 10 to 15m in length is normally sufficient. The athlete is kept in the starting position by an assistant to be released after the command "go".

The exercise assists in performing more active movements in the first phase of the start and can be performed outdoors or in a sports hall. (The rubber cords act as a break after the athlete has passed the posts).

Exercise 6:

The exercise requires a metronome to set an audible rhythm guide. The length of the strides is marked to stop the athlete shortening his strides in order to increase movement speed.

The exercise allows the development of the correct rhythm and tempo in the start.

Exercise 7:

Starting on a sloping track with a decline that does not exceed 3 to 5° in order to avoid changes in the running technique. The exercise is used to improve the rate of acceleration in the start.

Exercise 8:

Starting on an uphill track with an incline that does not exceed 5 to 10°. The run must be performed with a maximal movement ampliltude in shoulder and hip joints. The placement of the feet has to occur on the toes without the heel touching the ground.

The exercise is used to develop an active knee lift and to increase the stride length in the start. It is also useful in improving power.

Exercise 9:

Performed with a rubber cord, attached to connect the ankles of the athlete. The rubber cord is 40 to 50cm long, depending on its tension and the athlete's leg length. Markers are used to control the stride length.

The exercise allows the performance of active movements and obstructs jumping out of the blocks.

Exercise 10:

This exercise requires a weight belt and markers for stride length. The weight belt is about 3 to 7% of the athlete's body weight and should not distort the

movements or produce excessive strain. The height of the markers is chosen to assist in an active knee lift. The exercise requires sufficient ankle and lower leg strength.

Exercise 11:

An exercise that dictates active movements in the initial starting phase. The athlete, feet on the starting blocks, leans forward without touching the ground with his hands. He is held in this position by a short rope in the hands of the coach, who releases the rope on the command "go". The athlete, in order to avoid falling, is forced to lift his knees rapidly. The markers make sure that a correct stride length is employed.

The exercise helps to develop a fast and coordinated arm movement. However, care must be taken not to lean too far forward as this can lead to a fall or force the athlete to lift his shoulders and head to avoid it.

Exercise 12:

Similar to Exercise 11. The sprinter is held in an extended forward lean position by ropes in his hands. The ropes are released after the command "go". A flexible cord, attached to two posts, placed 2 to 3m from the blocks, helps to keep the lean and avoids an early straightening.

EXERCISE 1

EXERCISE 2

EXERCISE 3

EXERCISE 4

EXERCISE 5

EXERCISE 6

EXERCISE 7

EXERCISE 8

EXERCISE 9

EXERCISE 10

EXERCISE 11

EXERCISE 12

NEW APPROACHES TO SPRINT TRAINING

by A. Lavirenko, et al., and V. Breizer, et al., USSR

Although assisting and resisting training methods to develop stride length and stride frequency in sprinting have been known for some time, the following two texts present some new aspects, looking into studies to determine the most effecient methods and presenting a novel approach in using parachutes to provide constant resistance.

NON-TRADITIONAL TRAINING

A. Lavirenko, J. Kravtsev, Z. Petrova

The use of non-traditional training allows the increase of the intensity of sprint training in order to improve the level of muscular power, while the development of movement speed continues. The employment of such training means as running against resistance and the assisting towing method have so far been rather limited. For this reason we have studied both methods and can now make certain recommendations.

It is advisable, when using counter resistances, to keep these within 5 to 8% of the sprinter's body weight. This allows the performance of running at the restricted speeds with the same structure as running at maximal speed while at the same time developing specific muscular power. The "critical exertion" can under these circumstances exceed the normally developed power in the driving phase by 8.6%. The duration of the checking and amortization phase is now reduced and the running speed drops by about 12% through the shortening of the running strides (8%) and the reduction of stride frequency (3%).

Counter resistances over 8% of the athlete's body weight requires more driving power and lengthening the amortization phase. In addition, the take-off angle of the drive is changed; the stride length is reduced by 12% and the stride frequency by 6.5%. All this is responsible for a notable change in the structure of running technique and therefore not recommended.

Running under advantageous conditions by using a towing belt is particularly helpful for the development of maximal sprinting speed. The towing force should be 2 to 3kg and the towing speed 0.5 to 1.0m/seconds faster than the athlete's own maximal speed. Towing by this force reduces the duration of amortization by 11% and the time of the take-off drive by 3.5%. The driving force is somewhat increased. The running speed increases by 5% through a 2.2% lengthening of the running stride and a 2.6% increase of the stride frequency.

Towing forces exceeding 3kg are responsible for disturbances in the movement coordination. The body lean is increased, feet are "hammered" to the surface, the breaking time and amortization time are increased and the driving force is reduced.

Other interesting information was revealed by an attempt to determine the optimal running conditions by "interrupting the dynamics" of the run. This test began against a counter resistance that was broken off when the athlete had gathered speed. The athlete now continued with suddenly increased speed, thus allowing the determination of the influence of the exercise on speed and strength components. The results showed that a better training effect was achieved when the initial counter resistance was 5 to 11% of the athlete's body weight.

It was further discovered that following the break-off of the resistance the vertical checking and support forces that occur during the placement of the foot on the surface were reduced. The take-off, on the other hand, takes place with an increased horizontal force (5.7%). The support phase is lengthened, the flight phase reduced by 12.1% and the time over the control distance is naturally improved (2.4%).

The improvement of running speed in the interrupted resistance exercise occurs due to an increased stride frequency (.4%). The immediate training effect in a run that follows under normal conditions is reflected in a shorter support (3.2%) and flight (2.6%) phases. The horizontal support force is increased by 1.9%, the stride frequency by 2.4%. Although the stride length is reduced by 0.7%, the time over the control distance was improved by 1.9%.

Recommendations

Based on the above summarized results, it appears that the following recommendations are in order for qualified sprinters:

- Counter resistance runs with 5 to 8% of the athlete's body weight can be included in the initial and final mesocycles during the general preparation period over distances of 60 to 100m. The resistance runs take place twice a week in a microcycle. Athletes perform 1 to 2 runs against the resistance, followed by a single run under normal conditions. Recoveries between the runs are 2 to 3 minutes and 3 to 4 series are executed in one training session.

- The "interrupted dynamics" runs are incorporated in the training program during the second half of the general preparation and the beginning of the specific preparation period. Running is performed over 60 to 80m in 2 to 3 series in which two runs are "interrupted" and one is performed under normal conditions. Full recoveries are employed with the next run started when the heart rate has been reduced to 115 to 120 beats a minute. The athlete executes 5 to 6 standing starts and 2 to 3 varied speeds runs over 80 to 100m prior to the "interrupted" runs. Each weekly microcycle includes 2 to 3 sessions of such training.

- Counter resistance runs during the specific preparation period are performed over 80 to 100m distances. Each series consists of two resisted and one under normal conditions runs, performed in 2 to 3 series. Full recoveries, with the pulse rate 115 to 120 beats a minute before the next run, are again employed. The athlete executes 4 to 5 standing starts and 3 to 4 varied speed runs over 80 to 100m prior to the counter resistance runs. Each weekly microcycle includes 2 to 3 sessions of such training.

- Towed runs are incorporated in the training during the competition period. The towing speed should exceed the athlete's maximal speed by 0.5 to 1.0m/seconds. The athlete performs 3 to 4 series of runs, consisting of one towed run and one run under normal conditions. The distance is 80 to 100m and full recoveries are employed. Each weekly microcycle includes 2 to 3 sessions of such training.

RUNNING WITH A PARACHUTE

by V. Breizer, B. Tabatshnik, V. Ivanov

One principle to improve the efficiency of training is to increase the intensity with means that bring it close to the competition performance. This, for sprinters, is running at speed close to that of racing. However, this type of intensive but monotonous training creates psychological and physical fatigue. In addition, running at sub-maximal and maximal speeds stabilizes movement indicators and, after some time, restricts the transfer to higher speeds. That is the reason why a variety of training loads are employed, using assisting conditions combined with normal ones.

We create resistance by using a parachute, a training method originally employed by ice speed skaters. The parachute has an advantage in providing constant resistance in the horizontal direction and is attached close to the athlete's center of gravity. It can be used in running on the straight, as well as around a curve. In addition, parachutes are easy to make, they are light and take little space.

The dome area of a parachute, attached by ropes to the belt of the athlete, can vary between 1 to 3 square meters. According to our information, a parachute with a one square meter dome area has a breaking force of 4 to 5kg at running speeds of 9 to 10m/seconds. Two parachutes of the same size creates a resistance around 9 to 10kg. We experimented with breaking variations that corresponded from 7 to 15% of the athlete's body weight in the development of starting acceleration, maximal speed and speed endurance.

In the development of maximal speed and acceleration the athlete uses a standing start for 5 to 6 repetitions of 80 to 100m with 6 to 8 minutes recoveries between repetitions. The distances can be slightly longer, taking into consideration that the rate of acceleration with the parachute from a standing start is reduced and it requires 20 to 30m before the actual work begins.

Choice of Variations

Knowing that the use of a parachute will change the running technique, we employed only combined variations that included running with a parachute and running under normal conditions. Our experiments concentrated on the following three combinations:

- Three runs with a parachute, followed by 2 to 3 runs under normal conditions.

- Alternate runs with and without a parachute.
- The athlete drops the parachute at the halfway mark and completes the distance without it.

We selected finally the first variation as the most effective. It appeared to have two advantages, namely:

1. The combination of the two types of runs provided the best effect because the athlete "remembered" the driving force and direction in the runs with the parachute. Once released from the resistance the memorized action was immediately transferred to the free running performance.

2. A subjective factor also is involved. The athlete, after being suddenly unrestricted, feels free and has the desire to move his legs faster. In other words, the athlete desires to increase his running speed.

The development of starting acceleration with the parachute takes place from the crouch start. The parachute, attached to the belt of the sprinter, is placed on the ground next to the starting blocks. In a full effort crouch start the parachute opens at about the 10m mark (the speed corresponds to 80 to 85% from the maximum) and the sprinter continues to accelerate against the resistance. The distance for this exercise ranges from 30 to 50m. Two to three series are performed with 3 to 4 minute recovery intervals between the repetitions, 5 to 6 minutes between the series. The total volume is around 300 to 450m.

The development of speed endurance with the parachute can be based on two different approaches:

- Reducing the recovery intervals
- Increasing the running distances.

In the first case distances from 80 to 100m are employed in 3 to 4 series with recovery intervals of 3 to 4 minutes between the repetitions and 8 to 10 minutes between the series.

In the second approach the optimal distance appears to be 150m, performed in 5 to 6 repetitions with a 90% effort. Longer distances, 200 to 250m, are responsible for an early fatigue.

During the strength endurance training phase in March, for example, two parachutes were used to perform 4 to 6 repetitions of 150m. After an 8 to 10 minute recovery a single run without the parachutes was performed. The time of the runs performed with the parachutes was 0.7 to 0.8 seconds slower from the runs under normal conditions.

The resistance was reduced in April, according to the need to develop speed. The training had the following structure:

2 x 150m with two parachutes (0.7 to 0.8 seconds slower from the runs without a parachute).
2 x 150m with one parachute (0.3 to 0.4 seconds slower for the runs without a parachute).
1-2 x 150m under normal conditions.
Recoveries between the series 8 to 10 minutes.

Runs with the dropping of the parachute after the first 50m were introduced in May and continued. The pattern was as follows:

1 x 150m with two parachutes.
1-2 x 150m with one parachute.
2 x 150m with dropping of the parachute.
1 x 150m under normal conditions.

TRAINING FOR THE 400M

by William Black, USA

An outstanding review of the physiological factors of performance in the 400. The author does an excellent job of relating the physiological factors to the all-important aspect of race distribution. Black is affiliated with Performance Fitness of Cincinnati, Ohio.

Perhaps no other event is as perplexing to track coaches as the 400 meter dash. In contrast to a wealth of information about middle and long distance running and runners (Carter, et. al., 1967; Wyndham, et. al., 1969; Bosco, Komi, and Sinkkonen, 1980; Pollock, Jackson, and Pate, 1980; Taunton, et. al., 1981; Boileau, et. al., 1982; McKenzie, et. al., 1982; Conley, et. al., 1984; Svedenhag and Sjodin, 1985; Bale, Bradbury, and Colley, 1986), there is a lack of scientific information about the immediate and long term effects of competition and training and the characteristics of outstanding 400 meter performers. This makes it difficult to make a rational decision about the best methods for training for this event.

In order to answer the question of what is the best method for training 400 meter runners, it is necessary to analyze the nature and demands of the race by determining: 1. the responses to competition; and, 2. the characteristics of 400 meter competitors of varying levels of ability. The following information, derived from available literature, can be used as the basis for the rational planning of more effective training programs for the purpose of improving 400 meter racing performance.

During 400 meter racing, energy is derived from; 1. the breakdown of high energy phosphate compounds (20-25%); and 2. the anaerobic productions of ATP by glycolysis (55-60%), and 3. aerobic production of ATP (15-25%). (Gladrow, 1983; Daley, 1978). Of the standard running events the 400 probably requires the greatest energy production via anaerobic glycolysis, as evidenced by the observation that the most pronounced cases of lactate acidosis in athletic competition occurred after 400 and 800 meter racing.

Following a 400 meter dash of 45.5 seconds, an international caliber runner had a lactate concentration of 24.97 mmol/liter with a pH of 6.923 and a base-excess of 30.0 mval/liter. (Kindermann and Keul, 1977). Similar lactate concentration and pH values were reported following a run of 47.8 seconds (Osnes and Hermansen, 1972).

Research (Schnabel and Kindermann, 1983) indicates that the anaerobic capacity of runners is influenced by: 1. the energy derived from the lactacid anaerobic system; 2. energy derived from the alactate anaerobic system; and, 3. energy derived from aerobic metabolism. Those three factors were found to account for 57, 31, and 5% of the variability between groups of 400 meter, middle distance, long distance, and marathon runners in a short duration run to exhaustion.

The most pronounced difference between 400 meter runners with a mean best time of 45.6 seconds, and those with a mean best of 48.0 seconds was that the better 400 runners apparently produced more energy via the alactate anaerobic energy system. Although the apparent difference did not reach statistical significance, this finding led the researchers to hypothesize that the superior 400 meter runners may be characterized by "an extraordinarily high capacity to increase their alactacid anaerobic capacity."

Lending support to this observaiton is the finding of Jolly and Crowder (1985) that trained sprinters were able to both accelerate and maintain maximum velocity for a greater distance than untrained sprinters with similar maximum velocity capabilities, leading to the hypothesis that the trained sprinters may have increased levels of PC in the working muscles which extends the time before energy is supplied by anaerobic glycolysis.

The research of VanCoppenolle (1980) found that:

1. 400 meter dashes run in 43.8-44.9 seconds were accomplished by running the first and second 200 meters in a mean time of 21.5 (20.7-22.4) and 23.0 (22.1-23.5) seconds, respectively. 400 meters run in 45.0-45.9 seconds were run with the first and second 200s covered in mean times of 21.7 (20.8-22.7) and 23.8 (22.5-25.0).

67

The top runners have a smaller time differential between the first and second 200 meters (1.5 versus 2.1 seconds). The difference between the mean times for the second 200 meters for the two groups of runners is significant on the 1% level.

2. For the fastest (43.8-44.9) runners, there is no distinct correlation between the second 200 meters and the final time. A favorable result can be run with a relatively fast or slow second 200 meters.

3. For 400 runners in the 45.0-45.9 second category, there is a distinct correlation between a better final time and a better second 200 time.

This information indicates that the difference between the best and the sub-best 400 runners is that the best were able to run a faster second 200. It is not known whether that ability was due to: 1. a greater alactate; 2. a greater lactacid anaerobic capacity; 3. to a combination of the two factors, 4. which of the two made the most significant contribution to the running performance.

Taking into account the research of Schnabel and Kindermann (1983), it is possible that the ability of the top 400 runners to run a faster second 200, due to a smaller difference between the times for the first and second 200s, may be because the top runners derive more energy for running the first half of the race from alactate sources, thus reducing the detrimental effects of lactate acidosis on the running of the second 200.

The world record of 43.86 for the 400 was run at an average velocity of 9.10 meters/second. The mean stride length was 2.20 meters and mean stride frequency was 4.13 strides/second. The corresponding velocity, stride length, and stride frequency for a 100 meter dash of 9.95 seconds was 10.1 m/sec., 2.25 meters, and 4.40 strides/seconds, respectively. (Scholich, 1978). The first 200 was run in 20.7+ seconds and the second in 23.1+ seconds (Van Copponolle, 1980).

Ogorodnikov (1978) determined that 400 sprinters with best performances of 45.5 or better, 45.6-47.0 and 47.1-48.6 differed in their sprint speed abilities. The runners in these categories had mean best 100 times of 10.31, 10.52 and 10.78, respectively. It was concluded that "the sprinting ability of athletes was the single most important factor in the development of specific performance ability of the 400 meters. . . (and that) optimal training must be directed towards the development of speed."

Crielaard and Pirnay (1981) found that sprinters (including one 400 meter runner) developed much higher alactate anaerobic power values (1,030 W. or 14.16 W/kg) than 800 meter runner (761, 10.63), a long distance runner (551,

8.93), or student (710, 10.1) groups. Additionally, a strong negative correlation was found between maximum oxygen uptake and alactate anaerobic power in the athletic, but not the student, groups. The authors theorized that this relationship was due to: 1. the neural stimulation (fast twitch versus slow twitch) and enzyme activities (glycolytic versus oxidative) of muscle fiber; and, 2. the influence of different types of training.

Schnabel and Kindermann (1983) recorded mean maximal oxygen uptakes of 60.6 ml/kg/minutes and 59.5 ml/kg/minutes for groups of sprinters with mean bests for the 400 of 45.6 and 48.0 seconds, respectively. A 400 runner with a best of 46.7 had a reported aerobic power of 55.2 ml/kg/minutes (Withers, et. al., 1977). This compares to a mean of 56.15 ml/kg/minutes for world class sprinters with a mean 100 time of 10.23 (10.16-10.31) (Barnes, 1981) and means of 63.6 and 69.8 ml/kg/minutes for national class (1:49.5-1:53.7) Canadian and Finnish 800 runners (McKenzie, et. al., 1982; Rusko, et. al., 1978). Long distance runners had reported mean maximal oxygen uptakes in the high 70s (Boileau, et. al., 1982; Costill, et. al., 1973; Rusko, et. al., 1978).

On the basis of the available information, it is possible to conclude that:

1. Success in the 400 is highly dependent upon a very high ability to produce energy via anaerobic glycolysis, with the accompanying lactate acidosis. When comparing heterogeneous groups of runners, the anaerobic capacity of the athlete is the main determinant of superior ability to run the 400.

2. More successful 400 runners are characterized by superior sprint speed. When comparing homogeneous groups of runners characterized by a very high anaerobic capacity those who are faster over shorter distances tend also to be faster in the 400.

3. More successful 400 runners may be characterized by superior alactate anaerobic capacity. It may be that those runners who are able to produce more energy in the early stages of the race, via the splitting of high energy phosphates, are more successful.

4. Successful 400 runners are characterized by an anaerobic power similar to that of other athletes who participate in sports requiring a combination of speed and aerobic endurance (for example, soccer and basketball). A very high maximum oxygen uptake is not advantageous, and may even be detrimental, to high level performance.

Consequently, those training methods that most effectively increase the athlete's alactate anaerobic power and capacity and the capacity of the lactacid anaerobic energy system will produce the fastest times. The challenge to the coach and the sports scientist is to discover those methods.

REFERENCES

1. Bale, P., D. Bradbury and E. Colley, "Anthropometric and Training Variables Related to 10km Running Performance," *Brit. J. Sports Med.*, December, 1986; 20(4), pp. 170-173.
2. Barnes, W., "Selected Physiological Characteristics of Elite Male Sprint Athletes"; *Journal of Sports Med. and Physical Fitness*, 1981, 21, pp. 49-54.
3. Boileau, R., J. Mayhew, W. Riner and L. Lussier; "Physiological Characteristics of Elite Middle and Long Distance Runners", *Canadian Jour. of Appl. Sport. Sci.*, 1982, 7(3), pp. 167-72.
4. Bosco, C., P. Komi and K. Sinkkonen, "Mechanical Power, Net Efficiency and Muscle Structure in Male and Female Middle Distance Runners", *Scand. J. Sports Sci.*, 1980, 2(2), pp. 47-51.
5. Carter, J., F. Kasch, J. Boyer, W. Phillips. W. Ross and A. Sucec; "Structural and Functional Assessments on a Champion Runner—Peter Snell", *Research Quarterly*, 1967, 38(3), pp. 355-65.
6. Conley, D., G. Krahenbuhl, L. Burkett and A. Millar, "Following Steve Scott: Physiological Changes Accompanying Training:", *The Physician and Sportsmedicine*, Jan., 1984, 12(1).
7. Crielaard, J. and F. Pirnay, "Anaerobic and Aerobic Power of Top Athletes", *Eur. Jour. of Appl. Physiol.*, 1981, 47, pp. 295-300.
8. Jolly, S. and V. Crowder, "The Energy Continuum and the Stages of Velocity in Sprinting:", *Track Technique,* Winter, 1985, 91, pp. 2909-11.
9. Kindermann, W. and J. Keul, "Lactate Acidosis with Different Forms of Sports Activities", *Canadian Jour. of Applied Sport Sci.*, 1977, 2, pp. 177-82.
10. McKenzie, D., W. Parkhouse and W. Hearst, "An Anaerobic Performance Characteristics of Elite Canadian 800 Meter Runners", *Canadian Jour. of Applied Sport Sci.* 1982, 7(3), pp. 158-60.
11. Ogorodnikov, A., "Only A Lap—400 Meters" in *Sprints and Relays.*
12. Osnes, J. and L. Hermansen, "Acid-Base Balance after Maximal Exercise of Short Duration", *Jour. of Appl. Physiology*, Jan., 1972, 12(1), pp. 59-62.
13. Pollick, M., A. Jackson and R. Pate, "Discriminant Analysis of Physiological Differences Between Good and Elite Distance Runners", *Res. Qtrly. for Exerc. and Sport.*, 1980, 51(3), pp. 521-32.
14. Rusko, H., M. Havu, and E. Karvinen, "Aerobic Performance Capacity in Athletes", *Eur. Jour. of Appl. Physiol.*, 1978, 38, pp. 151-59.
15. Scholich, M., "East German Study of the Distance Stride", *Track Technique*, Winter, 1978, 74, pp. 2355-59.
16. Schnabel, A. and W. Kindermann, "Assessment of Anaerobic Capacity in Runners", *Eur. Jour. of Appl. Physiol.*, 1983, 52, pp. 42-46.
17. Svedenhag, J. and B. Sjodin, "Physiological Characteristics of Elite Male Runners In and Off-Season", *Can. J. Appl. Sport Sci.*, 1985, 10(3), pp. 127-33.
18. Taunton, J., H. Maron and J. Wilkinson, "Anaerobic Performance in Middle and Long Distance Runners", *Can. J. Appl. Sport Sci.*, 1981, 6(3), pp. 109-13.
19. VanCoppenolle, H., "Analysis of 200 Meters Intermediate Times for 400 Meters World Class Runners", *Track & Field Qrtly Rev.*, Summer, 1980, 80(2), pp. 37-39.
20. Withers, R., R. Roberts and G. Davies, "The Maximum Aerobic Power, Anaerobic Power and Body Composition of South Australian Male Representatives in Athletics, Basketball, Field Hockey and Soccer", *Jour. of Sports. Med. and Phys. Fitness*, 1977, 17, pp. 391-400.
21. Wyndham, C., N. Strydom, A. Van Rensburg and A. Benade, "Physiological Requirements for World Class Performances in Endurance Running", *S. African Med. Jour.*, Aug., 1969, 19, pp. 996-1002.

CHAPTER III:
THE FEMALE SPRINTER

TRAINING PROBLEMS IN WOMEN'S SPRINTING

by N. Sultanov, USSR

The author sums up various studies by the Soviet Union authorities into the long range development problems of women sprinters, concentrating mainly on the improvement of specific power.

Today's scientific literature devoted to sprinting is extensive, however, it covers mainly work done with male and not female athletes. Such a lack of information has often been responsible for planning of training programs that fail to take into consideration the differences of the female capacities. For this reason we will present in this article some experimental data on the training of girls and women.

DEVELOPMENT TRENDS

A study by Galukhin of women sprinters, who have clocked 10.8 to 11.1 seconds for the 100m, shows that all of them produced excellent results in their very first races (average time 12.63 seconds). During their entire career (7 to 9 years) they succeeded in improving their initial times by an average of 1.44 seconds. This indicates that maximum speed capacities are to a certain extent limited genetically.

The author also presented interesting data in comparing the multi-year growth of results of the best Soviet and foreign sprinters. It showed that the Soviet sprinters were significantly behind their foreign counterparts of the same age groups (0.29 seconds). Despite the fact that they had reduced the difference by the age of 16, their best achievements as a rule by the age of 22, were 0.32 seconds behind the world's best (1975 to 1976). All this indicates that talent search is a necessary prerequisite for the development of high class sprinters.

Galukhin added to this a pattern of the multi-year improvements in sprinting results and certain anthropometric data, based on a large group of outstanding sprinters. It provides a valuable reference point for model characteristics, as well as the development of long term training plans (Table 1).

In his study of 1500 girls in the 12 to 13 years age range, who had previously not participated in sport, Bogdanov discovered that only 13 girls had a support phase of their running stride in the 0.93 to 0.105 seconds range and a time of 5.0 seconds over 30m from a crouch start. It stressed once more the importance of the evaluation of sprinting capacities of children. Some values for these and other tests are shown in Table 2. In addition, the author found that kinematic characteristics of the running stride are directly related to the proportions of the body and its extremities, showing that individual traits of physique make the development of different techniques possible.

Table 2: Evaluation of sprint capacities of 12 to 13 year old girls.

Test	Evaluaton		
	Poor	Good	Excellent
St. Triple Jump (cm)	540	600 (+)	620 (+)
St. Long Jump (cm)	160	200 (+)	210 (+)
30m Bouncing (sec)	7.8	7.7 (-)	7.1 (-)
30m Bouncing (no. of strides)	16	15.5 (-)	14 (-)
30m from crouch start (sec)	5.2	5.0 (-)	4.9 (-)
25m from flying start (sec)	3.6	3.4 (-)	3.3 (-)
Support phase (sec)	0.115	0.105 (-)	0.100 (-)

Table 1: Multi-year changes in sprint results.

Distance	Best (sec)	Height (cm)	Weight (kg)	PB Age (yrs)	First Competition Age (yrs)	Time to Achieve PB (yrs)
100m	11.19	168 ± 1.2	58.3 ± 1.3	20.6	14.6	7.4
200m	22.40	169 ± 1.1	59.2 ± 1.5	21.7	14.6	8.7

SPECIFIC POWER

Various aspects of physical and technical developments of women sprinters at various ages were studied by Trubinkov, Bartenev and Semenov. Trubinkov determined that the running speed of young sprinters, who began training at the age of 11, increased from 3.92 to 4.50 m/sec until the age of 13. Then until the age of 15, it decreased to 4.20 m/sec before it began to improve again to reach 4.49 m/sec at the age of 17. The stride length, on the other hand, increased constantly with the age, reaching 1.77 m at the age of 17. These findings revealed the effectiveness of developing speed qualities in training during the adolescent and teenage years.

The author considers it important to employ repeated execution of general and specific power development exercises, as well as speed drills under normal, more difficult and lightened conditions. Most important in speed development are power exercises identical to running at top speed (bouncing and jumping exercises with or without weights, specific running exercises, exercises with medicine balls, sandbags, etc.). Speed development has proven to be most effective when dynamic exercises are used for power training.

Galukhin's work shows further refinement of this type of training. He determined that variations of methods establish a better base for the development of speed and speed endurance. Galukhin found that the optimum ratio for 14- to 15-year-old girls consisted of 70% of the workouts made up from specific power exercises and sprinting under more difficult and lightened conditions, while 30% of training used for sprinting under normal conditions.

Bartenev, studying the relationships between sprint performances and the development of physical capacities of women athletes, has come to several conclusions. He found that there was no correlation between sprint times with body weight and height. Tall girls had advantages only in the 14 to 17 years age range. A closer tie is found in the relative (not absolute) muscular strength and sprint results. Here the strength of plantar flexors of the foot, thigh extensors and flexors, extensors of the lower leg and the total of these measures, is closely related to sprint performances.

TRAINING METHODS

In recent times more attention has been paid to the finding of the most efficient methods of training in the sprinter's multi-year preparation. Studies

11.12/23.04 sprinter Natalya Kovtun, USSR

have shown that the correct use of training methods depends on a detailed study of bio-dynamics of the various methods and their correspondence with structure of sprinting. Bartenev worked out precise characterization of the principal sprint training methods in order to solve this problem and compared the results with various characteristics of running at maximum speed. By using this information it is possible to make purposeful changes in the dynamics, rhythm and structure of the individual exercises to fit the characteristics of sprinting. Particularly valuable are exercises and sprinting under lightened conditions, which enable the athlete to exceed maximum speed and lead to an increased movement frequency.

Semenov, studying the functional improvement of the motor system of women sprinters, found that

73

it is determined by the nature of work in running training. In his opinion sprinters do not succeed in reaching their potential maximum motor force. The ability to develop quickly useful external force is therefore below their capacity and, even more important, below their ability to reach potential maximum strength output. The author concluded that the initial muscle strength should be regarded as one of the most important criteria in evaluating the specific power development of women sprinters.

Studies have shown that the functional specialization of a sprinter's support system occurs primarily by specific stimulation required for the performance of fast running. This makes it necessary to differentiate the tasks of specific strength training, taking into consideration the preparation level of an athlete. Thus, specific strength training for beginners should ensure the functional specialization of the prime mover muscle groups at an early training stage. This muscular development must correspond with the demands of speed running to ensure a quality coordination of the main muscle groups

TRAINING MODES

A long experimental study allowed Semenov to recommend training modes that correspond fully to the demands of sprinting. These could be basically divided into the following three groups:

1. Bouncing from single leg take-offs, including triple and quintuple jumps, depth jumps with a forward and upward rebound, repetition jumps over obstacles, etc.

2. Bouncing from alternate leg take-offs with different arm actions over distances ranging from 50 to 200m. The explosive driving action is forward with an energetic knee lift of the leading leg (highly qualified athletes use thigh weights).

3. Strength exercises with weights or other resistances. Three to five slow repetitions with a heavy resistance is used for the development of absolute muscle strength. Explosive power is developed by fast movements with a resistance 40 to 50% of the maximum (8 to 10 repetitions per set) and muscular endurance by a large number of repetitions (15 to 20) with a resistance 10 to 15% of the maximum. Isometric exercises with a tension at 80% of the maximum are also used without holding of the achieved tension for long.

A YEAR'S TRAINING PROGRAM FOR WOMEN SPRINTERS

by Irena Szewinska, Poland

Irena Szewinska, the legendary world record breaker and Olympic champion of Poland, presents a detailed year's sprint training program in five main phases and their tasks for female sprinters.

A year's training program for sprinters is divided into the following five main periods:

1. Winter preparation period (10 weeks).
   Cycle 1—introduction to training (2 weeks)
   Cycle 2—main preparation phase (6 weeks)
   Cycle 3—pre-season training (2 weeks)
2. Indoor competition period (5 weeks)
3. Spring preparation period (10 weeks)
   Cycle 1—main preparation phase (6 weeks)
   Cycle 2—pre-season training (4 weeks)
4. Summer competition period (18 weeks)
   Cycle 1—first competition phase (6 weeks)
   Cycle 2—training phase (3 weeks)
   Cycle 3—second competition phase (9 weeks)
5. Transition—active rest period (6 weeks).

INTRODUCTION TO TRAINING

The weekly training program of this phase is based on the following: Monday—general strength, Tuesday—endurance, Wednesday—general strength, Thursday—endurance, Friday—general strength, Saturday—endurance, Sunday—rest.

The general strength development program employs loads that do not exceed 60% of the athlete's body weight (about 40kg.). The exercises are selected to develop all major muscle groups. About 10 exercises are performed in one training session in 6 series of 10 to 20 repetitions. A typical choice, for example, is made up of the following:

Bench press, abdominal exercises, clean, half-squat, back, hamstring and quadriceps exercises, medicine balls work, squats with 40kg, stretching exercises.

The development of endurance usually takes place outdoors and begins with an approximately 30 minute warm-up. The main part of the workout consists of 8 to 10 repetitions of two-minute easy runs with 2 to 3 minute recoveries and concludes with 10 minutes of jogging.

MAIN PREPARATION PHASE I

The weekly training program of this phase is based on the following nine units: Monday—strength, Tuesday—speed and technique/general preparation, Wednesday—endurance I/strength, Thursday—jumping exercises, Friday—endurance II/strength endurance, Saturday—endurance III, Sunday—rest.

The strength development program employs loads up to 90% of maximal strength, performed in 4 to 6 series of 3 to 20 repetitions. A typical workout consists of the following:

Bench press, abdominal exercises, clean (up to 30kg), split jumps with bar on the shoulders (up to 30kg), half-squat jumps with a bar (up to 40kg), arm technique work with dumbbells (2.5kg), squat (40 to 60kg), half-squat (70 to 100kg).

Speed and technique training employs sprints and drills to develop technique with maximum relaxation. This includes relaxed accelerations, starts from different positions, flying start sprints at $3/4$ speed and several other technique drills. Power speed exercises take place in the last phase of a warm-up and include skipping, bounding, high skipping, hopping and high hopping over distances of 20m. The running distances to develop speed don't exceed 60m and are performed relaxed with gradually increased intensity but without timing. Full recoveries are allowed between repetitions.

The general preparation sessions are made up from strengthening exercises, specific flexibility exercises, medicine balls work, hurdling and so on. All these exercises are performed in a dynamic rhythm.

The three endurance workouts are based on the following:

Endurance I—8 x 250m varied speed (100m sprinting + 50m jogging + 100m sprinting) at a comfortable speed with 3 minute recoveries. Endurance II—8 x 1 minute runs (approximately

300m) with 2 minute recoveries after each repetition and a 4 minute recovery after the fourth repetition. After three weeks the workouts are changed to 300m repetitions with the same recoveries. Endurance III—8 series of 5 x 100m interval running with 3 to 4 minute recoveries between the series.

Quantity, not quality is important in the development of endurance in this training period. It is the number of repetitions that counts, not the intensity of the work. Recoveries are short but the heart rate should not be higher than 120 to 130 beats a minute when the next repetition is started.

Jumping exercises include 6 x 10 repetitions of full squat jumps, 6 x 20 repetitions of bounding from one leg to the other, 6 x 20 hops on the right leg, 6 x 20 hops on the left leg, 6 x 30m of high stepping (L-R) and 6 x 10 repetitions of double legged jumps.

Strength endurance training consists of skipping 2 x 40m, 2 x 60m, 2 x 80m, 2 x 100m, 2 x 120m, 1 x 100m, 1 x 80m, 1 x 60m and 1 x 40m with short walk recoveries. Emphasis is on the technique and rhythm of the performance.

PRE-SEASON TRAINING I

Prior to the start of the indoor competition season the weekly training units are reduced to six: Monday—strength, Tuesday—speed, Wednesday—endurance I, Thursday—speed, Friday—endurance II, Saturday—rest, Sunday—time trial.

Strength training loads remain in the up to 90% of the maximum range, performed in series of four with 3 to 10 repetitions. For example: abdominal exercises, split jumps with up to 30kg, half-squat jumps with up to 25kg, hopping over 20m with an up to 20kg bar, full squats with up to 60kg, half-squats with up to 100kg. Easy running and stretching exercises complete the workout.

In comparison to the previous period several changes take place in speed training. These include starts with the gun, time control in repetition runs and increased recoveries between repetitions. A speed session, for example, can be made up from 4 to 6 starts from the blocks over 20m without commands, followed by 6 to 8 starts over 40 to 60m with the gun and 4 to 6 flying start sprints over 40 to 60m.

Endurance development workouts are also changed. Endurance I sessions consist of 6 to 8 series of 3 x 100m interval running with 3 to 4 minute recoveries between the series. The second endurance session uses 4 to 6 repetitions of timed 150m with 6 to 10 minute recoveries. Power speed training includes skipping, bounding, high hopping and uphill accelerations.

The contents of training during the indoor competition season is similar to the work employed during the pre-season period but the volume is reduced and tests are replaced by competitions. The indoor competitions help to prepare for the outdoor season and provide a break from intensive training. The races also help to improve sprinting technique and the crouch start, as well, as provide feedback on the efficiency of the training performed in the previous periods.

MAIN PREPARATION PHASE II

This training phase is divided into two cycles of which the first lasts six weeks and employs a large training volume. The weekly training program is based on the following nine units: Monday—strength/endurance I, Tuesday—speed, Wednesday—jumping/general preparation, Thursday—endurance II, Friday—strength/strength endurance, Saturday—endurance III, Sunday—rest.

The strength development program is similar to that used in the first main preparation phase.
The number of series and repetitions remain unchanged but an effort is made to perform the exercises more dynamically. During the second pre-season phase that follows, the number of repetitions is reduced and such exercises as the squat and the half-squat are limited to only 1 to 3 repetitions with a maximal or sub-maximal load.

Speed training concentrates on 40 to 60m sprints from a flying start, starting from the blocks over 20 to 40m and technique development drills. General preparation sessions include flexibility exercises, hurdling, medicine balls work and other track and field events.

In the three endurance development categories, endurance I is used as relaxation running after strength training. It usually includes 6 series of 3 x 100m with 3 to 4 minute recoveries between the series. Endurance II begins with 6 to 8 repetitions of 200m with 6 to 8 minute recoveries. The repetitions are timed and the intensity is gradually increased. This routine is changed in the pre-season cycle to 4 to 6 repetitions of timed 150m with 8 to 10 minute recoveries.

Endurance III sessions consist of 8 x 300m with 4 minute recoveries and 4 x 300m with 10 minute recoveries. Time trials replace the 300m runs in the pre-season cycle of this period. The time trials alternate between 2 x 300m in the first week and 2 x 200m in the second week. The time trials alternate between 2 x 300m in the first week and 2 x 200m in the second week. The recovery for 300m is 30 minutes, for 200m 45 minutes.

Irena Szewinska won three Olympic gold, two silver and two bronze medals during her 16-year international career as a sprinter and long jumper.

Strength endurance training follows closely the program employed in the first main preparation and pre-season phases. Jumping training is reduced

from 6 series in the first six weeks to 4 series in the pre-season cycle, using mainly 10 repetitions for each of the chosen exercises.

SUMMER COMPETITION PERIOD

As mentioned in the introduction, the 18-week long summer competition period is divided into two competition cycles separated by a short 3-week training phase. The following training programs are employed:

Competition phase I: Monday—endurance I, Tuesday—strength, Wednesday—speed, Thursday—endurance II, Friday—rest, Saturday—rest, Sunday—competition.

Strength training in these phases stresses dynamic exercises, using up to 12kg heavy sand bags for hopping and bounding. Half-squats are performed with sub-maximal loads in series from 5 to 1 with 4 to 2 repetitions. Jumping exercises are performed in series reduced from 6 to 3 and include the standing long jump, standing triple jump, standing five jumps, standing 10 jumps and the squat and jump (10 repetitions). All jumping workouts are completed with 4 series of 4 x 50m sprints.

Speed training is similar to the pre-season cycle and usually consists of 6 to 8 repetitions of 20 to 40m starts from the blocks, followed by 4 to 6 repetitions of 20 to 60m sprints from a flying start. Some of the repetitions, but not all, are timed. Endurance sessions usually include 6 to 4 series of 3 x 100m interval sprints with 10 to 15 minute recoveries between the series.

The weekly training plan in the short training cycle, sandwiched in between the two competition phases, is based on the following eight training units:

Monday—strength/endurance I, Tuesday—speed, Wednesday—jumping exercises/strength endurance, Thursday—endurance II, Friday—strength, Saturday—endurance III, Sunday—rest.

The means of strength, speed, strength endurance and jumping development are similar to those employed in the second main preparation phase in the spring preparation period. However, there are some differences in the endurance workouts. Endurance I consists of 6 to 8 series of 3 x 100m interval sprints with 3 minute recoveries. Endurance I employs 6 to 2 repetitions of timed 150m with recoveries being increased from 10 minutes to 15 minutes and finally to 20 minutes. Endurance III is made up from 4 to 2 timed 300m repetitions with 15 minutes, 20 minutes and 30 to 45 minute recoveries.

THE SPRINTING STRUCTURE OF FLORENCE GRIFFITH JOYNER

by A. Levtshenko, USSR

A detailed examination of the technique and the racing structure of Seoul Olympics triple gold medallist and world record holder Florence Griffith Joyner, looking at her sprinting action with an analysis of velocities, stride length and stride frequency.

Florence Griffith Joyner (169cm tall, weight 59kg) was born on December 21, 1959, in Los Angeles. Her first outstanding success in elite sprinting came in the 1984 Olympic Games where she collected the silver medal in the 200m. However, she remained in the shadow of the best German Democratic Republic's speedsters, Gohr and Drechsler, as well as the United States' Ashford during the next two years.

It was in 1987 that Joyner gave a warning of her true intentions when she dashed to a personal best and a silver medal in the World Championships in Rome. Next year she made experts think twice about the limits of female sprinters when she turned in a sensational 10.49 second World Record in the United States Olympic Trials in Indianapolis, cutting 0.27 seconds(!) off the previous mark. It was followed by three golds and a silver medal at the Seoul Olympics, including another sensational world 200m record.

SPRINTING TECHNIQUE

The following analysis of Joyner's sprinting technique is based on a film sequence taken in the 200m final in Rome in 1987, where she finished second to Gladisch of GDR in a time of 21.96 seconds. Although not comparable with her 21.34 seconds in Seoul, there appears to be no notable differences as far as her sprinting technique is concerned. This applies particularly to our analysis of the characteristics of a single phase of the running stride at full speed.

FOOT PLACEMENT

The support phase begins with an elastic placement of the front part of the foot of a nearly straight leg in the knee joint. The angle of the foot is about 64° to the track, with the lower leg in a position that is close to the vertical. The heel is kept well off the track (Figure 1a). This action allows a foot placement close under the vertical projection from the athlete's center of gravity to the track, while a relatively high heel position secures amortization at the landing.

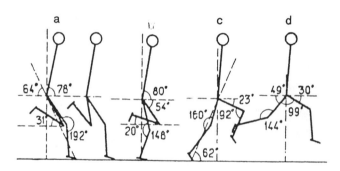

Figure 1: An analysis of Joyner's sprint technique

The last is responsible for the energy accumulation in the muscles and ligaments of the lower leg that can be exploited in the next phase. It also should be noted that the angle between the thighs is minimal, an indication of an active swinging leg movement. The body, with relaxed shoulders, has a 12° forward lean.

THE SWINGING LEG

The angle of the bend in the swinging leg at the moment the lead leg is placed on the track to start the support phase is approximately 31° (Figure 1a). The heel of the swinging leg is below the level of the athlete's seat. As this indicator is usually within a 36 to 42° range for female sprinters, it can be said that Joyner's leg bend has been relatively small.

Joyner brings the heel of a bent swinging leg in a smooth trajectory fast underneath the seat, without an excessive knee lift. The fact that the angle between the support and the swinging legs at the beginning of the support phase is minimal has to be stressed (Figure 1a). The thighs are virtually parallel at this moment and allow Joyner to perform a very fast and effective short lever forward swing, followed by an efficient breaking action. It is technically regarded as a very important element of the sprinting technique.

THE LANDING

The angle in the knee joint at the vertical moment of the landing is about 148° and the thigh has an optimal forward lean of about 10° (Figure 1b). This is optimal to all well qualified sprinters and characteristic of a "high" landing. A rigid placement of the leg to the track, with an optimally small amortization in the knee joint secures here an optimal amortization in the ankle joint (Figure 1b). This is followed by a fast and powerful drive, making use of the elastic capacities of the foot, lower leg and thigh muscles (Figure 1c)

THE DRIVE AND FLIGHT

Joyner's takeoff drive is performed at an angle of about 62° with an approximately 160° angle in the knee joint. At this stage the world record holder's indicators are again optimal and correspond to most highly qualified sprinters, who have a driving angle in the range of 60 to 64°. A straightening of

the knee joint at the moment of the takeoff is not justified. This would lead to an unnecessary "idle gear" that slows down the following bending knee action (Figure 1c).

Joyner's flight phase is executed in a manner that resembles an energetic jump with the lead leg's thigh about 30° to the horizontal plane and an angle of approximately 99° between the thighs (Figure 1d). This, once more, is regarded as optimal. The flight action is brisk with a slight raise of the center of gravity. The position of Joyner's body is close to vertical and the amplitude between her thighs is sufficiently wide before they move fast closer in the following phase.

THE ARMS

Finally a few remarks on Joyner's arm action, although it is generally accepted that the movement of the arms has no direct influence on running speed. Joyner's upper and lower arms are well coordinated, moving practically parallel. The movement amplitude is wide and both arms reach a virtually stretched position at the start of the support phases.

STRUCTURAL INDICATORS

Videos taken in 1988 show that the basic elements of Joyner's sprinting technique have not changed, although her action has become stronger

Table 1: The structure and basic indicators of Griffith Joyner's 100 and 200m races at Seoul Olympics.

Average Indicators	100m			200m		
Time (sec)		10.70	10.54	21.56	21.34	
Velocity (m/sec)	0-30m	7.89	8.02	8.46	8.48	0-50m
	30-60m	10.53	10.71	10.10	10.22	50-100m
	60-100m	10.81	10.96	10.06	10.16	100-150m
	0-100m	9.64	9.84	9.43	9.54	150-200m
Stride Length (m)	0-30m	1.73	1.73	1.86	1.86	0-50m
	30-60m	2.31	2.29	2.26	2.25	50-100m
	60-100m	2.40	2.40	2.33	2.32	100-150m
	0-100m	2.11	2.12	2.34	2.34	150-200m
Stride Frequency (stride/sec)	0-30m	4.56	4.64	4.55	4.56	0-50m
	30-60m	4.56	4.68	4.47	4.53	50-100m
	60-100m	4.50	4.57	4.32	4.36	100-150m
	0-100m	4.55	4.62	4.03	4.08	150-200m

Florence Griffith Joyner at the 1988 Olympic Games

and more powerful. Joyner herself said in an interview that her improvement has occurred mainly from a larger training volume and better quality strength development. According to her statement the training volume was in 1987-88 increased by up to four times.

The structure and the essential basic indicators of Joyner's 100 and 200m races at the Seoul Olympic Games are presented in Table 1 and Figure 2.

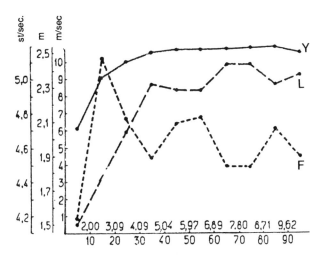

Figure 2: The structure of Joyner's 100m final 10.54w at Seoul Olympics. Velocity dynamics = (V); stride length= (L); stride frequency = (F)

THE 100m

Joyner has frequently stated in her interviews that she used to watch the videos of Johnson's and Lewis' performances at the Rome World Championships and attempted to copy the first in the start and the second in full speed running. Looking at the information presented in the table and the graph indicates that she has solved the task successfully.

Joyner's fast reaction time of 0.131 seconds (Johnson 0.129 seconds) is followed in the start by a powerful drive from the blocks and in the first 3-4 strides. Her stride length continues to increase as she reaches the 30m mark in an excellent 4.09 seconds. Specialists usually claim that Joyner's stride exceeds that of her rivals. However, she executed the acceleration from the blocks with "normal" strides, attempting to exploit the advantages of stride frequency.

Her first 30m was covered in 17.8 strides of an average length of 173cm. This means a relative stride length of 1.02 (the average stride length over the first 30m divided by the height of the athlete),

which supports the statement that Joyner's starting acceleration was performed with "normal" strides. Practically all top sprinters—Ashford, Drechsler, Nuneva, Gladisch—have in 0.99 to 1.02 a similar relative stride length coefficients.

At the 30m mark Joyner appeared to smile, as if the outcome of the final was practically decided. Her sprinting action became more powerful, the running stride lengthened considerably and the stride frequency dropped. Joyner reached her maximal velocity between 60 and 90m, where she covered three 10m sections in 0.91 seconds, and at some stage apparently reached speeds exceeding 11 m/sec.

Her average stride length in the 30 to 60m section was 2.29m (relative—1.36), in the 60 to 80m section 2.44m (relative—1.44). These coefficients indicate an "extended" stride length, turning the sprint into what resembles a series of bounds. It is interesting to note here that Lewis, who is 188cm tall, had in the Rome 100m final an average stride length of 2.44m. The coefficient of the relative stride length of the best female sprinters (Ashford, Kondratjeva, Gladisch, Drechsler, etc.) ranges between 1.25 and 1.35.

Joyner was only 0.01 seconds slower over the last 10m than her fastest sections between 60 and 90m. This indicates a very high level of specific endurance that is apparently the result of the development of strength endurance in the major muscle groups. As can be seen in the table, Joyner improved her 10.70 seconds in the semifinal to 10.54 seconds in the final by increasing the stride frequency in all sections. At the same time her stride length remained unchanged. She took 47.6 strides in both races with an averge stride length of 2.11-2.12m.

THE 200m

In the Olympic 200m final Joyner's reaction time was 0.205 seconds, considerably slower in comparison to the 100m. The same applies to her average running speed that reached its peak at 10.16 m/sec. between 100 and 150m. This was 92% of the fastest section in the 100m final. Joyner's stride frequency in the 200m dropped from section to section and was below the 100m indicators in all but the starting acceleration part-distance. Her speed, in comparison to the fastest section (100 to 150m) dropped over the last 50m by approximately 7%. The number of strides in the final and semifinal (21.56 seconds) remained practically unchanged at 91.8 strides. The faster time in the final was achieved mainly by an increased stride frequency in all sections.

SOME FEATURES OF WOMEN'S TRAINING

by Tiina Torop, USSR

The author discusses the anatomical and physiological differences of women that influence training procedures concentrating on strength and power development as one of the most important factors to improve performances.

The comparison of men and women in sport leads frequently to emotional views that women should copy everything that men are doing in training to get as close as possible to the performance capacity of males. While there are several common aspects that apply to both sexes in sport, it should nevertheless be understood that a women is not a scaled down man. What follows in this text is therefore an attempt to discuss some of the anatomical, physiological and psychological differences of the females in sport.

MENSTRUATION

Neal of the United States has correctly claimed that the understanding of women's sport is badly influenced by traditionally biased views. Among them for a long time was an understanding that training and competing during menstruation is harmful for the organism. Marker, for example, discovered in a study conducted in 1925 that only 6% of the 15,000 athletes surveyed trained during menstruation. The situation today is reversed.

It is actually interesting to note the fact that women have been frequently responsible for personal best performances during menstruation. According to Tosetti, Fanny Blankers-Koen of Holland set seven out of her nine world records in sprinting and hurdling in the 1940's and 1950's during her menstruation. Kindermann of the University of Freiburg has stated that the work capacity of women does frequently reach its maximal indicators during menstruation.

Of course, there can be individual problems as shown in a survey conducted by Jagunov and Stratseva. Their results indicated that 81.6% of women athletes turned in normal or better performances during menstruation, while 18.4% were below their normal standard. The authors did consequently divide women into the following four groups:

Group 1 (55.6%) is made up of athletes who in all phases of their menstruation felt well and, according to functional tests, were capable of high level performances.

Group 2 (34.5%) includes athletes who during menstruation suffer from a hypnotical syndrome, characterized by general weakness, fatigue and unwillingness to train.

Group 3 (5.1%) includes athletes who suffer from a heavy hypnotical syndrome, characterized by irritability, sometimes lack of coordination and difficulties in relaxing. Some suffer from stomach aches, headaches and sleeplessness.

Group 4 (4.9%) is made up of athletes who suffer from lack of appetite, muscular aches, faster pulse rates and increased breathing rates.

As can be seen, the reaction of the organism to menstruation can differ considerably, making it clear that athletes in the first group can train and compete during menstruation, while those belonging to the last three groups should avoid training and competition at this stage.

PHYSICAL DIFFERENCES

The body proportions of men and women are different. Women have a longer upper body and shorter legs, lowering the center of gravity 6% below that of men. This is responsible for a better balancing capacity but reduces movement speed and jumping height. Women also have narrower shoulders and wider hips.

The muscles of women are less developed and

usually do not exceed 35% of the total body weight, compared with 40 to 45% for men. According to Letunov, 28% of the weight of women is made up from fatty tissue, while the average for males is only 18%. This means that women have 10 to 15% less active muscle mass and about 10% more passive fatty tissue. However, there are exceptions and Nett has drawn attention to the long legged, narrow hips and lean female athletes who represent better potential. This applies particularly to the development of such physical capacities as speed, strength and power, as women are considerably weaker than men in abdominal, shoulder and leg muscles.

Better joint mobility and flexibility, on the other hand, make it easier for women to perform movements that require a large amplitude. They also have advantages in events that require precise coordination because women adjust themselves better to timing and movement rhythm. Anokina, for example, claims that elite women track and field athletes are characteristically capable of using their coordination and joint mobility to determine closely their performance effort. She also claims that girls are more efficient in technique development, provided the learning procedures are adjusted to their work capacity.

Their learning procedures should therefore employ running at reduced speed, hurdling over low hurdles (50 to 60cm) with shorter distances (6.5 to 7.0m) apart, high jumping according to their ability, etc. As far as hurdling is concerned, it should be kept in mind that girls are often hindered by fright. Courage must therefore be taught as part of hurdles training, combined with a large number of different jumping exercises over a variety of obstacles.

TRAINING PROCEDURES

There has been a lot written about the differences in the training procedures of men and women, although the information often lacks specificity. While very little help was available from sport scientists in the early days of women's athletics, contemporary information indicates that, despite the specific features of the two sexes, the main principles of training apply to both. The differences occur only in the contents, volume and intensity.

Training in track and field events assumes the performance of an enormous volume of running and jumping exercises. This requires the development of leg strength, particularly in the ankle and lower leg. Weak ankles, according to the medical adviser of the Soviet athletic team, Dr. Vorobjov, are responsible for many injuries. The development of ankle strength should therefore take place practically in every training session throughout the athlete's career.

All-round strength development exercises have a most important place in the training of female athletes. Weaknesses in the upper body strength do not only influence throwing and jumping performances but also running. The main task of the upper body muscles is to establish a solid posture. The development of upper body strength should therefore be regarded as the first assignment for women athletes. It can also be said that the differences between men and women are particularly noticeable in strength, a factor to be taken into consideration in the choice of training methods, as well as in perspective planning.

The development of weak muscle groups should take priority during the first two or three years of training. It will be followed by the development of all muscle groups before the prime mover muscles will receive priority. The last takes place when high level specialization begins. Anokina recommends employing exercises that combine strength development with technique training in the early stages of strength development. The use of medicine balls is a typical example of how strength can be developed parallel to the other physical capacities and the techniques of several events.

The learning of the throwing events is particularly difficult for girls. There are subjective and objective factors involved. Holding of the shot with the upper arm at shoulder height, for example, can be extremely difficult. The relatively longer upper arm also restricts the final delivery speed. Lack of finger strength makes it harder to control the implement and the direction of the delivery.

STRENGTH DEVELOPMENT

Female athletes, regardless of their chosen event, should develop all muscle groups during the first phase of specialization. Additional loading is introduced at this stage, using a complex of 8 to 10 exercises that are performed in two or three series at the end of each training session. Each series is made up from 6 to 10 repetitions and stretching exercises between the series are not to be neglected.

Strength development in the next specialization stage, when the classical barbell exercises are added to the program, becomes extremely important. However, there are still contradicting views on how to approach this phase, particularly about the weight of the barbell and other resistances used. This writer would like to stress here once more the need for strong postural muscles before any barbell exercises are attempted.

Specific strength exercises at the high performance level are performed in virtually all training sessions (5 to 6 times a week) or in 2 to 3 separate training days. Exercises are performed in series where the number of repetitions is reduced as the resistance is increased and the recoveries are lengthened. Strength development should make up about 40 to 50% of the total training volume during the preparation period and takes place parallel to technique development.

Particular attention at this performance level is directed to event specific exercises. Bondarchuk stresses here that the only positive approach at the high performance level is to employ event specific exercises. General all-round strength development belongs to lower performance levels. This principle also applies to women athletes.

Finally, it is important to keep in mind in the planning of weekly microcycles that better results are achieved in technique and speed development when this work immediately follows a strength oriented training load.

Strength preparation during the competition season is nearly as important as during the preparation period, although the work volume and the number of training days are somewhat reduced. The employment of strength exercises is also recommended in pre-competition training, using 2 to 3 fast repetitions of each familiar exercise against low or medium resistances.

NOTEWORTHY COMMENTS

Czechoslovakian authority, Dr. Kral, who has thoroughly studied women's strength training, has made several valuable comments on the problems. He recommends that women athletes avoid the single maximal repetition method in weight training because of the stress on the lower part of the pelvis. The same applies to exercises where the resistance is restrained.

Women should take care in performing depth jumping exercises, a power development method widely employed by men. Depth jumps place extraordinary demands on the weaker joints and ligaments of women, who, for the same reason, should also use isometric exercises only on a limited scale.

In the performance of event specific exercises it is most important to preserve the movement structure and amplitude of the actual event. Restrictions to the amplitude and impediments to the rhythm are usually caused by excessive loading. Women must avoid this and should always strictly follow the principle of a maximum movement amplitude. Restrictions in the movement range strain ligaments and tendons, as well as affect the elasticity of the muscles. An increase in the overall load should therefore be first attempted through movement speed. Resistances can be increased only after adaption has taken place.

In summary, it can be said that women athletes should not be worried that strength development exercises will change their figure. They should instead keep in mind the importance of the strength component in the performance power and the length of time it takes to develop it.

SOME QUESTIONS AND ANSWERS ON WOMEN'S SPRINTING

by A. Levtshenko, USSR

Leading USSR coach Levtshenko answers a series of questions related to women's sprinting, covering such factors as the speed dynamics, stride frequency, stride length and the useful indicators for the monitioring of training.

QUESTION 1

There is sufficient information available on the speed dynamics, stride length and stride frequency of male sprinters but it appears that the technical literature is short of similar data on female sprinters.

In the 100m sprint it is possible to divide the distance into four parts that reflect the efficiency of the performance of both male and female sprinters. These are the starting acceleration (0-30m), reaching maximum speed (30-60m), maintaining the speed (60-80m) and the finish (80-100m), each showing its own speed dynamics, stride length and stride frequency. Based on this information it is possible to establish a model for women sprinters for the achievement of a particular performance under 12 seconds (see Table 1).

Most important are the indicators at 30m, 60m and 80m because they allow the coach to:

- compare the actual time of each phase with the planned time
- predict the 100m time, based on the splits of the short phases
- discover the strong and weak aspects of a sprinter by comparing the individual split times with the model for necessary adjustments in training.

For example, shortcomings in the first phase indicate the need to concentrate more on starting and initial acceleration. Shortcomings in the second phase show poor maximal speed and in the fourth phase the lack of speed endurance.

The running speed over the total distance and in each phase is decided by the stride length and the stride frequency.

In the starting acceleration phase (0-30m) the leading component, responsible for an increase in the running speed, is the stride length. The

Table 1: Model split times for women's 100m sprint.

100m time	Split times						
	0-30	0-60	0-80	30-60	69-80	80-100	60-100
11.00	4.20	7.07	9.01	2.87	1.94	1.99	3.93
11.10	4.23	7.13	9.09	2.90	1.96	2.01	3.97
11.20	4.25	7.18	9.17	2.93	2.01	2.05	4.06
11.40	4.31	7.30	9.32	2.99	2.02	2.08	4.10
11.50	4.35	7.35	9.40	3.00	2.05	2.10	4.15
11.60	4.38	7.41	9.48	3.03	2.07	2.12	4.19
11.70	4.41	7.47	9.56	3.06	2.09	2.14	4.23
11.80	4.43	7.52	9.63	3.09	2.11	2.17	4.28
11.90	4.46	7.58	9.71	3.12	2.13	2.19	4.32
12.00	4.48	7.63	9.79	3.15	2.16	2.21	4.37
12.10	4.51	7.69	9.87	3.18	2.18	2.23	4.41
12.20	4.54	7.75	9.95	3.21	2.20	2.25	4.45
12.30	4.56	7.80	10.02	3.24	2.22	2.28	4.50

average stride length in this phase for high level women sprinters is 1.89 relative units (relative to leg length).

In the maximal speed phase (30-60m) the stride length reached at the 30m mark is 2.35 relative units and remains virtually unchanged. At the same time, the stride frequency is the highest and becomes the leading component in the increase of speed in this phase. The stride frequency improves 10% here in comparison to the acceleration phase.

The beginning of fatigue in the maintenance of the maximal speed phase (60-80m) is responsible for compensating changes in stride frequency and stride length. This is expressed in the lengthening of the support and flight phases, during which the stride frequency drops on an average by 2 to 5% and the stride length increases by the same percentage, reaching 2.43 relative units. The running speed is therefore basically maintained.

The sprinting structure continues to change in the finishing phase (80-100m) as fatigue increases. Running speed drops by 3 to 4% in comparison to the previous phase (60-80m), stride length increases by 2 to 6%, reaching 2.46 relative units and stride frequency drops by 1 to 9%.

QUESTION 2

Sprint coaches have for a long time discussed the best type of women 100m sprinters. Tabatshnik, for example, separates the "powerful short striding" GDR sprinters from the "relaxed and easy" running types, like Ashford and Kondratyeva. What can be said about this?

In my opinion it is possible to divide the women sub-12 second sprinters into several groups. Each of these groups has a leading performance component, depending on the natural characteristic to cover the distance with "short" or "long" strides, as well as their approach to training in order to develop their individual potential. Let me explain how the sprinters belonging to the various groups differ.

The first group is made up from relatively short athletes (160 to 168cm), who employ a "powerful" action with relatively short strides and a high stride frequency. Their average stride length relative to their height is 1.12 to 1.16. A typical example of this group is Gohr of the German Democratic Republic.

Taller athletes (170 to 180cm) usually belong to the second group and employ a diametrically opposite action with long strides and relatively lower stride frequency. The average stride length relative to their height is over 1.22. A typical example is Marshall of the United States.

The majority of women sprinters belong to a group in between the first two (80%). They are from 157 to 180cm tall with a more balanced relationship between stride length and stride frequency. Their average stride length relative to their height ranges between 1.16 to 1.22. An example is Ashford of the United States (see Table 2).

None of the groups appear to have an advantage and athletes in all three can succeed, provided their training is based and oriented towards the development of the athlete's natural potential.

QUESTION 3

Correct training is responsible for a steady improvement of sprint results. What are the basic indicators that change and decide the improvement in performances?

The split times improve in all the separate phases of the 100m distance due to an increased stride frequency. The stride length has less influence and only in the first two phases. Most improvements are achieved by the coach's ability to exploit the athlete's natural potential:

1. By increasing the stride length and stride frequency.

2. By reducing one component and increasing noticeably the other component.

Table 2: Sprint indicators of top sprinters in the different groups.

Athlete	Year	Height (cm)	Weight (kg)	100m time (sec)	No. of strides	Length of strides (m)	Frequency (stride/sec.)
M. Gohr (GDR)	1986	165	55	10.91	55.8	1.81	5.22
S. Gladish (GDR)	1987	163	57	10.82	51.7	1.95	4.88
H. Dreschler (GDR)	1986	181	70	10.91	46.5	2.17	4.32
E. Ashford (USA)	1986	165	54	10.91	52.0	1.94	4.83
A. Nuneva (Bul)	1987	167	63	10.92	50.0	2.01	4.69
M. Zirova (USSR)	1987	170	59	11.22	50.0	2.02	4.56

Table 3: Decisive indicators in improved performances.

Athlete	100m		0-30m			30-60m			60-80m			80-100m		
	Time	Stride No.	1	2	3	1	2	3	1	2	3	1	2	3
A. Nuneva (Bulgaria)	11.40	52.5	7.61	1.62	4.70	9.84	2.00	4.92	9.95	2.05	4.85	9.66	2.15	4.56
	10.92	50.0	7.91	1.74	4.55	10.34	2.14	4.83	10.36	2.15	4.82	10.20	2.20	4.64
N. Zirova (USSR)	11.50	49.6	7.55	1.81	4.17	9.80	2.06	4.76	9.80	2.20	4.45	9.62	2.19	4.39
	11.22	49.9	7.78	1.81	4.30	9.86	2.05	4.81	10.26	2.22	4.62	9.90	2.18	4.54

1 = Speed (m/sec); 2 = Stride length (m); 3 = Stride frequency (stride/sec.).

Some examples of the changes in competition sprint structure related to improved performances are shown in Table 3. As can be seen an increased stride frequency helped to improve the time (Zirova), while a drop in stride frequency, due to a longer stride, can be helpful in other situations (Nuneva).

QUESTION 4

How can a coach make use of the presented information?

The reply to this question can be given by a concrete example of how a competition model is worked out:

Sprinter M: 100m result in 1987—11.99 sec.

Plan for 1988—11.80 sec.

Leg length—0.87m

Distance from the line to the back block—0.70m.

We take the model indicators in Table 1 for the 30m, 60m and 80m phases that correspond to the planned time. The average speed in the starting acceleration phase is:

$$\frac{30m + 0.7m}{4.36 - 0.26} = 7.49 \text{ m/sec.}$$

30.7m is the distance of this phase from the back block;

4.1 seconds is the actual time allowing 0.25 to 0.29 seconds for the reaction to the starting gun.

The running speed required for the other phases can be calculated in a similar manner.

To determine the average stride length for each phase it is necessary to know the athlete's leg length (measured standing from the ground to the center of the head of the femur). The leg length is multiplied by a corresponding co-efficient M (stride module = the relationship between the stride length with the leg length). The co-efficient for high level performers vary between 1.88 and 1.89 for the first phase, 2.34 and 2.36 for the second phase, 2.43 and 2.46 for the third phase and 2.39 and 2.48 in the fourth phase, depending on their performance standard.

For our model calculation in the starting phase:

Average stride length—0.87m x 1.89 = 1.64m

Number of strides (0.30m)—$\frac{30.7}{1.64}$ = 18.7 strides

Average stride frequency —

(0.30m)—$\frac{7.49 \text{ m/sec}}{1.64\text{m}}$ = 4.57 stride/sec.

The stride length and stride frequency for the other phases can be calculated in a similar manner.

The planned model has to be compared with the sprint structure of the previous season, taking into consideration the individual's realistic potential to increase stride length, to increase stride frequency, to improve the acceleration from the start and to improve and maintain speed in the second half of the race. This naturally requires precise information on the sprint structure in major competitions by making use of electronic timing and video or film from each of the phases.

Finally, it should be kept in mind that the use of the average indicators in the establishment of a model for top level athletes is not always effective. Far more effective in these situations is concentrating, not on the weaknesses of the athlete concerned, but on the development of her strong points. These, however, are usually already well above the average indicators. While concentrating on the strong points, the weaknesses are not to be overlooked. They must at the same time be developed to reach the average indicators level.

UNIVERSITY OF TENNESSEE WOMEN'S SPRINT TRAINING PROGRAM

by Bernie Dare, Beverly Kearney, USA

When Kearney and Dare were assistant coaches with the UT women's program they wrote this valuable overview of the system developed for sprint training. Here is helpful general and specific material for every coach, with a well-designed yearlong periodized program geared toward the U.S. college season.

GENERAL PHILOSOPHY

Within the limitations of our facilities, weather, environment, school calendar, and the scholastic and social demands placed on the athlete, we try to implement a training program that addresses:

1. The basic physiological and biomechanical needs of the sprints;
2. The more specific and individual needs as the athlete matures, progresses, and as we both (coach and athlete) learn about those individual responses to exercise.

We emphasize sprinting, and high speed sprinting, as the more event specific exercise and backbone of the training program, in all parts of the training year. Weight training and plyometrics are supplementary and secondary factors.

Our program has six major factors in six week training cycles with weekly microcycles, and periodize to provide peaking/resting periods prior to the major championships.

SPEED TRAINING

In any sprinting event, sprinting speed is the most important factor for predicting success. Even among 400m runners, it is usually the faster 400m sprinter who wins (other things being equal). Any human exercise, such as sprinting, is a holistic activity, and it is difficult to separate exercise into individual component parts. Nevertheless, for training purposes, we emphasize these separate components of sprinting speed development:

- sprinting ("full-speed," full recovery)
- relaxation
- power production

Sprinting, or absolute speed, can be trained through repetitions of short distances (30m-100m), done at or near full speed, in a relaxed manner. We emphasize relaxation in all of our speed training and do not want the athlete to strain to hold full speed (in training). We also emphasize variety in these sprint work intervals, which may help avoid a plateauing effect (stagnation) that is possible in repetitive exercise at the same intensity. These workouts are very similar to those used by Valentin Petrovski with Valeriy Borzov, and emphasize "complete" recoveries between repetitions and sets. Such recoveries are usually 3-4 minutes between reps, and 5-8 minutes between sets. Such long recoveries are used because fatigue is thought to be counterproductive to learning and developing intense neuromuscular movements.

The volume of work varies with the time of year and the athlete's ability to sprint fatigue and tension free, and would typically be between 6 and 16 repetitions spread over 2 to 4 sets.

Typical workouts include the following:

1. 3 x 100 to 90-95%
   3 x 60 to 99%
   3 x 30 crouch start, 99-100%
   3 x 30 crouch starts, 95%
2. 3 x 150 alternate 95% 30m with 75% 30m
   3 x 100 in-outs
   3 x 50 finish 50's (medium build-up with last 25m at 99-100%)
3. 4 x 100 at 90% (accelerate to 90%)

4 x 100 in-outs
6-8 starts alternating 100% for 15m with 100% for 30m starts.

In all cases, the athlete avoids sprinting with fatigue or tightness, remaining relaxed and loose, even if she has to back off a bit.

Relaxation and power production are part and parcel of good sprinting. They are covered in greater detail below. With respect to speed training, relaxation facilitates proper neuro-muscular recruitment patterns, and reduces antagonistic muscle activity, which can inhibit the contraction of the antagonists (those muscles performing the major work of the movement). Increased power increases speed by either increasing the number of muscle units involved in the contraction, or the strength of each involved muscle unit, both of which can result in increasing the force against the ground, which can result in a longer stride; or more importantly, if more force can be created in less ground contact time, less ground contact time and greater stride frequency (it is less ground contact time, therefore greater stride frequency, that separates good and great sprinters).

SPEED ENDURANCE TRAINING

Speed endurance, the ability to maintain high speed sprinting, has two metabolic facets:
1. Alactic speed endurance
2. Lactic (glycolytic) speed endurance.

Again, the body is a holism, and these metabolic processes are not absolutely separable, and training the lactic system certainly trains the alactic system. The alactic system, or short speed endurance, predominates in exercise through the 200m; although the lactic system, or long speed endurance, begins contributing to intense exercise after about 5 seconds and probably becomes the dominant system between 10 and 20 seconds of activity. Due to the different energy demands of the 100m-200m, or short sprints, and the 200m-400m, or long sprints, and the real differences between athletes who are good short sprinters and those who are good long sprinters, we separate the two in training (this is also done to reduce anxiety among the short sprinters who dread sprints above 300m in length). Although these workouts vary with the cycle we are in:
• Short sprinters do repetitions of 100-300m, with volumes of 2 to 10, depending on the length of the work interval and the intensity of the work interval (speed).
• Long sprinters do repetitions of 150-600m, with volumes of 2 to 12, with the same considerations as the short sprinters.

We categorize all of our speed endurance work as "interval" work, as there is a work interval (sprint) and recovery interval (rest) involved, rather than use the many other names (repetitions, extensive, intensive, etc.). Then, we categorize our interval work by the intensity (speed), duration (time or distance), and degree of total fatigue created by each work interval and the total workout. The volume of the workout is then determined by the contribution of each interval to the total fatigue of the lactic acid or alactic energy system. They tend to fall into three categories, with some overlap.

1. Low Anaerobic Stress Workouts.

Characterized by low to medium intensity, short to medium durations, low to medium stress or fatigue—they approach total fatigue slowly. These sprint workouts build up fatigue slowly, and are used with short recoveries between sprints (1-3 minutes, or 120 bpm heart rate). They are primarily used in the early cycles (prior to Christmas break) and may also be used for aerobic conditioning.

Examples:
• 3-4 x 150
• 3-4 x 100
• 3-4 x 50 to 90% with 1-2 min. between reps, 2-4 reps between sets
• 8 x 200 with 100 walk, 100 jog as rest (1-2 min.) at about 28-30 sec. each
• 10 x 150 accelerations to 90%, 1-2 min. rest
• 5-6 x 300 with 1-2 min. rest, slow (48-54)
• 5 x 200 with 3 min. rest, moderate (27-28)
• 6-12 x 400 fartlek (100 walk, 100 jog, 100 stride—65-70 pace, 100 sprint—90%
• 3-4 x 300-200, 1 min. between 300 and 200, 3-5 min. between sets, approximately 48-50 and 27-29.

2. Medium to High Anaerobic Stress Workouts.

Characterized by medium to high intensity, short to long durations, medium to high stress or fatigue—they approach total fatigue more quickly, each interval significantly contributing to total fatigue. These sprints are run at or near event race speeds, they build up fatigue quickly. Relatively complete recoveries (to 100 bpm HR) are used, as each interval contributes significantly to total fatigue. The recoveries may be long (10-30 minutes, or 120 bpm heart rate). They are primarily used in the early cycles (prior to Christmas break) and may also be used for aerobic conditioning.

Examples:
- 3-4 x 150
- 3-4 x 100
- 3-4 x 50 to 90% with 1-2 min. between reps, 2-4 reps between sets
- 8 x 200 with 100 walk, 100 jog as rest (1-2 min.) at about 28-30 sec. each
- 10 x 150 accelerations to 90%, 1-2 min. rest
- 5-6 x 300 with 1-2 min. rest, slow (48-54)
- 5 x 200 with 3 min. rest, moderate (27-28)
- 6-12 x 400 fartlek (100 walk, 100 jog, 100 stride—65-70 pace, 100 sprint—90%
- 3-4 x 300-200, 1 min. between 300 and 200, 3-5 min. between sets, approximately 48-50 and 27-29.

2. *Medium to High Anaerobic Stress Workouts.*

Characterized by medium to high intensity, short to long durations, medium to high stress or fatigue—they approach total fatigue more quickly, each interval significantly contributing to total fatigue. These sprints are run at or near event race speeds, they build up fatigue quickly. Relatively complete recoveries (to 100 bpm HR) are used, as each interval contributes significantly to total fatigue. The recoveries may be long (10-30 minutes), or progressive (5-8 min., 8-12 min., 12-15 min.—longer with each proceeding work interval). Complete recoveries are used when doing these workouts near championship meets (in peaking/resting phases).

Example:
- 3-4 x 300 (5-8 min. rest 39-44, depending on ability)
- 1 x 600, 1 x 500, 20-30 min. rest, very fast (1:30-1:38) 72-75)
- 500-300-200, progressive rests (72-75; 5-8 min.; 39-42; 8-12 min.; 24-25) or 500-300-200 with 5 min. rests (76-80, 40-44, 25-27)
- 3 x 200 at 99% with 10 min. rests
- 1 x 300, 10-20 min. rest
- 1 x 200 at 99%
- 2 x 300, 2 x 200 with 5 min. rests (40-43; 25-27)

3. *High Anaerobic Stress Workouts.*

Characterized by high intensity, medium to long durations, high to very high stress or fatigue—approach total fatigue very quickly—exhaustive workouts. These are very hard workouts and are not done in or too near a peaking phase ($1^1/_2$-2 weeks before Conference Championships). They are meant to simulate 400m race stresses and are not done more often than once a week (usually once every 2 weeks).

Examples:
- 300-200 at race pace for 400 with 1 min. rest, 20 min. rest, repeat or 2 x 200
- 1 x 500 at 99%, 20-30 min. rest, 1 x 300 at 99%
- 1 x 600 at 99-100%, go home
- 1 x 500 at 99-100%, go home

For the short sprinter:
- 1 x 200 at 99%
- 3 x 100 at 99%
- 3 x 50 at 99% all with 5 minutes rest.

In training speed endurance, we start with type 1 workouts and blend into type 2 workouts, done below (slower than) the ability of the athlete, in our cycles before Christmas break. After Christmas, we begin with type 2 workouts adding type 3 workouts when the athletes are ready for them. As we near championship meets, we eliminate the type 3 workouts and modulate the type 2 workouts (more rest, more speed). We do the harder workouts near the beginning of the week. We treat meets as hard workouts and have an easy or rest day after them.

WEIGHT TRAINING

Weight training has two major rationales:
1. To provide total body conditioning to prevent muscle imbalances
2. To provide general muscle-tendon-ligament strengthening to reduce injury and better perform workouts.

The second is to increase muscle group strength, through either increased recruitment of muscle fibers or strengthening of muscle fibers (both occur), to increase the ability to apply power to the ground.

Current training theory for weight training usually has the athlete begin with 8-12 repetitions of an exercise, proceeding to sets of 6 or less (at appropriate repetition maximums—RM's), as fast twitch muscle fibers are not significantly trained above 6 RM. Variety or set-rep changes are used throughout the year to avoid stagnation.

Maintenance work (3-4 sets of 5 reps, 1-2 x a

week) should be done in the peaking/resting cycles. Excluding warm-up sets, set-reps structure could look like this:

4-6 weeks general conditioning—
    3-4 sets of 8-10 reps.
normal six week cycles—
    4-5 sets of 5 reps
or 5-5-3-3-(3), or 5-5-3-2-3

peaking/resting cycles—
    3 sets of 5 reps 1-2 x week as able—in all other cycles lift 3 x week or 5 x over a two week period.

Currently, our lifts and time in the weight room are limited by pending construction. Too, the ideal weight program for the time available, facilities usage, and need of the events and athletes is evolving, and is expected to change over the next two years.

Current Program:
    Weeks 1-4 (Cycle I): 4 sets of 10 reps
    Weeks 5-9 (Cycle II): sets of 10-5-5-3-3-3
    Week 10 (end of Cycle II): Max in key lifts
    Christmas Break: as able.

This series is then repeated during the six week cycles (Cycles III and V), with a maintenance program during the peaking/resting cycles, (IV, VI). Weight lifted per exercise is expected to be progressive throughout the 5 weeks of 10-5-5-3-3-3, then maxed for 1 week, then going to a reduced resting phase (peaking/resting cycles).

The current lifts are:
- full squats (parallel)
- bench press
- arm curls
- tricep curl (French press)
- incline press
- leg press (machine)
- calf rise
- hamstring
- curl (machine)
- leg extension (machine)
- lunges

PLYOMETRICS

Done correctly, plyometric exercises are very intense and their major rationale is to try and increase the ability to apply force to the ground very quickly. Great sprinters are able to apply large force to the ground from small knee angles (less knee bend and less leg flexion throughout the force application) with short ground contact times. To attempt to train for this, plyometric activities should try to mimic such actions. They should be very fast with short ground contact times, and should use shallow knee flexion. Our current major plyometric activity was to be flying start, single-leg hops (20m sprint start, 30m hopping). However, the skill level of our athletes in performing this activity was not high enough, and a learning process is now occurring. Instead, we are doing more general plyometric work, including bounding, skipping, and hopping without a flying start (200-600m of varied activity). We do these once a week and intend to do them twice a week (1 x week fast plyometric activity, 1 x week general plyometric activity) when skill levels are increased (we wish to avoid injuries caused by the unskilled doing an explosive activity).

FORM WORK

Form work, or isolating and training various facets of sprinting form, has been a part of much sprint training. However, there are some questions as to its efficacy. Recent biomechanical analysis of arm motion, for example, has failed to find any great significance in the specifics of arm motion to sprinting ability. Earlier studies also point out that neuromuscular coordination is very specific to the speed of movement. That is, form work has to be done at event speeds to properly stimulate and train the event neuromuscular coordination (firing sequence of the muscles). Form work has the following purposes:

1. As a warm-up activity
2. To develop a feeling for muscle movements that can be transferred to high speed activity
3. To strengthen certain group muscles
    a. slower, rhythmical form sprinting loosens, stretches, and warms up the muscles for sprinting
    b. it can train the athlete to recognize what muscle groups are doing, and should do, during sprinting (of varying importance)
        • the relaxed and quick recovery of the foot and leg after ground contact, creating a short lever movement efficiency;
        • allowing knee lift to occur, as it will, without forcing it, or pre-empting it;
        • to drive or stab the foot quickly to and off the ground after knee lift has occurred
    c. the hamstrings, hip flexors and extensors, and ankle flexors can be strengthened.

Training examples:
- 3-5 repetitions over 30-100m for all drills
- fast high knee drill, small steps (1-2' length)
- high skips (emphasize ankle extension and hip extension—these are skipping strides with a large vertical movement)
- quick foot drill (start slowly and pick up speed with each quick foot movement—about every third stride stab the foot to the ground very quickly, after the completion of knee lift (do not pre-empt knee lift)—this is similar to a hurdler's trail leg drill except for the more normal motion of the "trail" leg—alternate legs—as speed, return to normal sprint motion and ease off).

We currently do such form work 3 x week as a warm-up acvitity and think of it as rhythmical plyometrics. Form work is probably best practiced as a holistic activity (the body acting as a coordinated whole) during near full speed and full speed sprinting. At speed, the athlete concentrates on relaxation, smooth, quick recovery, and getting the foot to the ground and off quickly after knee lift occurs.

Upper body relaxation can also be trained at the same time. It may be productive to emphasize individual form facets during acceleration and within a repetition, and then try to put everything together. Facets then can be emphasized:
- leg-foot drive
- leg pull through (recovery), allowing full knee lift
- stabbing the foot to the ground quickly, and upper body form and relaxation.

RELAXATION

"Relaxed" sprinters sprint better. Being able to return muscle contractions on and off very quickly is the essence of sprinting. As such, it allows the next contraction to take place without "tension", which can hinder the speed and force of the contraction. Relaxation probably has inherent or genetic factors, but it can be aided through training. Like any learning process, for relaxation to become second nature, it must be practiced, and concentrated on during sprinting. The athlete must concentrate on both individual muscle groups and total body relaxation.

This can be a part of everyday's sprinting.

There is a second factor to relaxation. This involves learning to relax and visualize the process of sprinting and the race (useful in all events). Perceiving a positive, successful performance reduces "race" tensions, anxiety, and any apprehensions. The procedure varies slightly, but it can proceed as follows, and can be done anytime, especially the day prior to or the day of competition:
- find a quiet, comfortable place
- lie down
- starting with the feet, contract and relax all the muscle groups alternately from toe to head
- relax the entire body
- visualize all aspects of the race in a positive way (winning—performing movements correctly) from warm-up to finish line).

If done with the aid of a coach, his or her use of a monotone, hypnotic voice is beneficial (see RELAX AND WIN, by Bud Winter). Relaxed, positive, pre-race visualization of the event has been shown to have a positive effect on the stopwatch.

TESTING

Tests for power, strength, speed, speed endurance, and starting mechanics can be useful in isolating weaknesses and individualizing the program to address such weaknesses. Currently, we use the following tests, and test at the beginning or end of each cycle, or as needed for each athlete:
- 30m flying start*—tests for speed
- 60m crouch start*—tests for speed endurance (alactic)
- 30m crouch start*—tests for starting mechanics
- 300m—speed endurance more specific to 400m
- body fat % (under water weighing)—tests for fat % and excess weight levels
- standing long jump—tests for power

*NOTE: We use the standards developed by V. Petrovski. For the other tests we either use our own standards or those developed by the USOC/TAC Elite Athlete project.

We are considering the use of other tests, as we determine those which are most predictive and beneficial to measuring and improving athlete performance.

We do not always give every test at each testing session/cycle. Rather we use athlete progress and performances to dictate the area of testing. Too, competitive performances often furnish better results in the competitive season than tests such as these. Some of the tests are given within a cycle when indicated (e.g., athlete weight gain, speed or speed endurance when a weakness is indicated). Unfortunately, good weather and good facilities are a must for comparing test results to standards. Therefore, we find meet results more useful during the early competitive season (late November to early April are our cool weather months).

The basic Petrovski standards are listed below. For a given performance expectation in the 100 or 200 all three measurements should be at the same level. When the 30m CS, 30m FS, and 60m CS are at different levels it indicates a weakness (or perhaps strength) in one or more of the areas.

30m FS	30m CS	60m CS	100m CS	200m CS
3.3	4.3	7.6	12.0	24.5
3.2	4.2	7.4	11.6	23.8
3.1	4.1	7.2	11.3	23.2
3.0	4.0	7.0	11.1	22.5
2.9	3.9	6.9	10.9	22.0
2.8	3.8	6.8	10.7	21.4
2.7	3.7	6.7	10.5	21.0
2.6	3.5	6.6	10.3	20.4
2.5	3.5	6.5	10.1	20.2

Standing Long Jump Standard: 8'2" or better.
Body Fat % Standard(s): 6 to 12%

SUMMARY AND PERIODIZATION

Coaching is a continuous learning process. We try to use the best available information and technology that can be used within the limitations of our facilities, competition calendar, scholastic/social demands and athlete ability to perform. We believe that sprinting is more important than other activities; and when time, weather, and facilities conspire, we slight those other activities, rather than sprinting. We also believe that a good basic program coupled with a good coach-athlete relationship can be more important than worrying about all the technical measurements and scientific feedback from those. We change the training program in response to new information, but within the training year. Unless there are serious contraindications, we make no substantial changes (i.e., we wait to the next year to evolve the program). We try to do those things that are most productive, and, due to time considerations and the ability or inability of an athlete's body to respond, try to avoid wasting time doing those things that have little impact on

sprinting (i.e., slow activities such as excessive aerobic conditioning, slow sprinting—contradiction in terms, or slow "power" movements—again a contradiction). We also believe that intuition and common sense are necessary in applying scientific knowledge to a particular training and competition program, and that the coach needs to develop an intuitive "feel" for each athlete and her ability to perform. Unfortunately, these intuitive and "feel" skills are difficult to define. With the accumulation of a great deal of technical knowledge by the coach, and with the experience of coaching the athlete over a period of time, an understanding of the athlete and her event can occur and this can be a key element in coaching that athlete. Intuitive logic also plays a key part in applying scientific knowledge to the field situation. Such scientific knowledge and measurements of performance can establish parameters within which a training program should be structured, but it cannot establish an exacting model that everyone can or must follow for ultimate success. The reasons for this are several (they are not innumerable):

1. Athlete's genetic variability will define that athlete's ability to respond to training, which might affect the specific exercises she can do, and the intensities and volumes of training she can tolerate.
2. Competitive calendars are created by schools and governing bodies often without regard to what is best physiologically and psychologically.
3. Weather and facilities can limit the implementation of the "best" training program.
4. Personal and social factors also affect an athlete's adaptation to training.

Because of these things, there will always be an inner and outer parameter within which the "best" training program can be found. It is up to the coach and athlete, intuitively, by feel or (horrors) by a bit of hit and miss, to find this "best" or "optimum" training program.

The periodization for the 1986-87 year follows. It is geared to the SEC/NCAA Championships. The transitions between cycles may be adjusted one week one way or the other, depending on athlete progress and weather. The activities within a week are scheduled to best fit the athlete's time and the availability of facilities. Specific workouts are adjusted, likewise to meet changing factors in the coach-athlete environment. We do certain types of workouts at certain times in each cycle. The exact workout may not be scheduled

TRAINING CYCLES: 1986-87

Dates:	Cycle:	Training Emphasis:	Training Days (per week)
Sept. 21 to Oct. 25	I 4-5 weeks	1. General Conditioning 2. Speed Development	2 days—speed development; 3 days—weights (4x10); 1-2 days — speed endurance (low intensity); 2 days—aerobic endurance; 1 day—play day.
Oct. 26 to Dec. 6	II 6 weeks	1. Speed 2. Speed Endurance 3. Technique 4. Power	2 days—speed/technique; 2 days—speed endurance (low to moderate intensity/stress); 3 days—weights (10-5-5-3-3-3); 1-2 days—plyometrics.
Dec. 7 to Jan. 3(7)	IIA	1. Maintenance and General Conditioning	Christmas break: varies with athlete's ability to train.
Jan. 4(8) to Feb. 14	III 6 weeks	1. Speed Endurance 2. Speed and Technique 3. Power	2 days—speed and technique 2 days—speed endurance (medium to high stress); 3 days—weights (10-5-5-3-3-3); 1-2 days—plyometrics; 1 day—rest/travel; 1 day—competition
Feb. 15 to Mar. 14	IV 4 weeks	1. Resting phase for Indoor Championships 2. Speed/Technique	2 days—speed and technique; 1 day—speed endurance (longer recoveries); 1-2 days—weights (maintenance); 1-2 days—rest/travel; 1-2 days—competition.
Mar. 8 to Mar. 21	IVA 2 weeks	1. Rest/Refreshing Cycle 2. Maintenance	2 days—speed and technique; 1 day—speed endurance (light); 1-2 days—weights (maintenance); 2-3 days—rest or light activity.
Mar. 22 to May 2	V 6 weeks	1. Speed Endurance 2. Speed and Technique 3. Power	2 days—speed and technique; 2 days—speed endurance (high); 3 days—weights (10-5-5-3-3-3); 1-2 days—plyometrics; 1 day—rest/travel; 1 day—competition.
May 3 to May 16(17)	VIA 2 weeks	1. Peaking/Resting for Conference 2. Speed and Technique	2 days—speed and technique; 1 day—speed endurance (fast, long recoveries; avoid high fatigue); 1-2 days—weights (maintenance); 2-3 days—rest/travel/light; 1-2 days—competition.
May 17(18) to May 23	VIB 1 week	1. Rest/Recovery 2. Speed/Technique 3. Maintenance	2 days—speed and technique (light); 1 day—speed endurance (light); 1-2 days—weights (maintenance); 2-3 days—rest or light.
May 24 to June 6	VIC 2 weeks	1. Peak/Resting for NCAA 2. Speed/Technique	2 days—speed and technique (fast and light); 1 day—speed endurance (fast, long recoveries); 1-2 days—weights (maintenance); 1-2 days—rest/travel/light; 2-3 days—competition.
June 7 to June 13	VID 1 week	1. Rest/Recovery 2. Speed/Technique 3. Maintenance	2 days—speed and technique (as needed); 1-2 days—speed endurance (as needed); 1-2 days—weights (maintenance); 2-3 days—rest or light.
June 14 to June 27	VIE 2 weeks	1. Peaking/Resting for TAC	2 days—speed and technique; 0-1 day—speed endurance; 0-2 days—weights (maintenance); 2-3 days—rest/travel/light; 2-3 days—competition.

ahead of time, but the intensity and duration of the workout are. We also expect the 6 week cycles to be progressive in intensity, with Cycle I and II being progressive in duration, while the others might be regressive in duration (volume).

SAMPLE WEEKS (MICROCYCLES)

Below are listed examples of workouts that correspond to the types of training for the cycles listed. They can be used as a general guide to what we do but the speed of our training programs are adjusted to take into account athlete recovery from workouts, facilities and weather, and the necessities imposed by meets and travel arrangements. Generally, such changes will be reflected in whether we do speed endurance on Monday-Wednesday, or Tuesday-Thursday, and which days we rest/travel.

Cycles I & II
Mon: Speed and technique work—6-12 reps of 30-150m; plyometrics—3x3x50m fast hops, or 200-600m general (bounding, skipping, hops).
Tues: Speed endurance—100-200: 4x300, 5 minutes rest; 200-400: 500-300-200 or similar; weights.
Wed: Light activity—e.g., basketball; stretch and jog; 6x100; rest.
Thurs: Repeat of Monday, for the most part; may wish to do plyos on Friday or Saturday; e.g., 3x100 accelerations to 90%, 3x100 in-outs, 6x30m starts.
Fri: Speed endurance—short sprinters: 6-8x400 fartlek; long: 8-12 x 400 fartlek, or 8x200.
Sat: Play day (alternate activity such as basketball, soccer, etc.); or interchange Friday and Saturday.
Sun: Weights on own.

Cycles III & V
Mon: Speed and technique—8-16 reps 30-100m;

plyometrics.
Tues: Speed endurance—short: 300-300-200-200, or 300-200; long; 500-300, or 300-200/300-200 1 minute/20 minute rests; or 600-500-300-200; weights.
Wed: Depends on recovery—light speed technique; general plyometrics.
Thurs: Speed technique or speed endurance as needed by athlete; weights (e.g., 6-8x200, 8x150, or 4x150, 4x100, 4x50).
Fri: rest/travel/light
Sat: Meet or time trial or speed endurance/speed technique as needed (light activity if needed).
Sun: Weights on own.

Peaking Cycles IV and VI
Mon: Speed and technique: 3x100, to 95%; 3x60m finish 60s; 6 x starts.
Tues: Speed endurance—3x200 with 10 minute rest at 99%, or 1x300/1x200, with 10-20 minute rest at 99%.
Wed: Light as needed, weights.
Thurs: Speed and technique: 6-10x30-100m.
Fri: Rest/travel if meet Saturday; light or rest if not.
Sat: Meet or as needed (e.g., 2x200 with 10-15 minute rest @ 95-99%).
Sun: Meet?? or light weights on own.

Mon: Light speed endurance—1x200 99%, 3x100 accelerations to 95% or in-outs, 3x50, 20m running start, 99%.
Tues: Speed technique as needed—8-12 reps 30-100m.
Wed: Travel/light shake-out: 6-8x30-60m accelerations to 90-95%.
Thurs: *Rest* or light speed technique: 6-8x30-60m.
Fri: Meet (Qualifying rounds?).
Sat: Meet (Finals).
Sun: Meet? Rest/travel?

CHAPTER IV:
TALENT DEVELOPMENT

THE YOUNG SPRINTER

by Hans Torim, Estonia, USSR

A series of recommendations on how to approach the development of young sprinters, looking at physical preparations and technique training.

Genetic factors are largely deciding, in not only the physique of an athlete, but also the other capacities that influence sprint performance. Among these inherited capacities are the movement reaction time, tolerance to oxygen debt, functions of the nervous system and also coordination and power. This gives sufficient foundation to the statement that good sprinters are born and the choice and identification of talent are extremely important.

However, talent is only a prerequisite and it has to be developed by a systematic approach to training that begins in a play format in the childhood.

Sufficient movement freedom in playful physical activities, combined with inherited characteristics, allow youngsters already at the age of 10 to establish running kinetics that are similar to top sprinters. The most decisive component of running speed, the stride frequency, is also best developed before the age of 12 to 13 years. The same applies to other factors, such as the speed capacity, power, flexibility and joint mobility.

Nevertheless, specific sprint training should not begin as early as possible. The long term preparation of sprinters must be organized so that the athlete reaches physical, technical and tactical maturity during the best physiological age. It is also important to realize that a sprinter will tolerate intense specific training and competition for only 7 to 8 years on the average.

PREPARATION STAGES

Keeping in mind the laws governing the physical and psychological development of youngsters, as well as the best ages for the development of certain capacities deciding the sprint performance, has led to a generally accepted long term preparation process. This plan divides the training and development of sprinters into several stages, each of which has a particular task with appropriate means and methods. The exact age boundaries for the separate stages and their duration might differ slightly between authorities, but the basic principles of the model remain common and are based on the following:

- The physical development of sprinters has to begin relatively early to avoid missing the favorable age periods for the development of important sprint performance capacities.
- The first preparation stage should be based on age specific exercises, means and activities, dominated by games and play methods.
- The general physical preparation in the first stages must be many-sided, using movement games, gymnastics, acrobatics and a variety of other sporting activities.
- The starting levels of capacities and abilities of the children should be established in the first preparation stage and their early progress monitored to evelute their suitability to a particular group of events.
- Emphasis on narrower sprint specific training means and methods is to be delayed and started relatively late.

The above listed principles stress the many-sided general physical development during the early years of training, followed by a gradual step by step change to sprint specific training and an increased training volume (Figure 1).

A correct approach to physical activities and training in the early preparation stages are decisive in the development of sprinters. Mistakes that are made here will later be almost impossible to compensate, therefore a lot depends on the theoretical and practical knowledge of coaches and physical education teachers involved with young potential sprinters. They must be patient and purposeful in their guidance and avoid looking for

Table 1: Training stages of a sprinter

STAGE	AGE	TRAINING DIRECTION AND CONTENTS	TASK
Introductory	6-8 to 11-12	Many-sided play methods	Finding of a suitable sport
Basic	11-12 to 13-14	Many-sided activities directed towards athletics	Finding of a suitable group of athletic events
Initial specific	15-16	Many-sided athletic activities in a group of events (sprint, hurdling, long jump)	Finding of a suitable sprint distance
Specific	17-18	Training and competing in sprinting events	Aiming for a performance in the main distance.

an early success at all costs. Consequently the practical, as well as theoretical and methodical, training of the coaches of young athletes must be far more many-sided than their counterparts in charge of adult athletes.

THE INTRODUCTORY STAGE

Regarded as the "playing years", the main tasks of this stage are:

- The many-sided development of physical capacities
- The development of many-sided skills and movement qualities
- The development of lasting interest in physical activities
- The initial direction towards the most suitable sport, based on the evaluation of the physical and psychological developments in the many-sided activities.

Basic Physical Preparation

This is a favorable age for the development of movement speed, movement frequency, agility and coordination. Emphasis is therefore based on movement games and sporting games with simplified rules, such as soccer, baseball, volleyball, handball and basketball.

Also important are gymnastics, acrobatics, rhythmic gymnastics for girls, skiing, ice skating and swimming. The learning of basic athletic skills of running, long and high jumping and throwing is a must. It is based mainly on games that involve the performance of running, jumping and throwing. Multiple event competitions are recommended towards the end of this stage.

The improvement of coordination is the prerequisite for the development of stride frequency and running speed. At this age coordination can be developed with any kind of

running and it would be wrong to assume that the improvement of speed capacities requires a lot of fast running. Slow running and different running speeds in playing games are as valuable as fast running.

Games and relays, involving on an average 15 to 30m repetitions, are excellent for the development of stride frequency and running speed, while reaction speed is developed in games where 5 to 15m repetitions are frequently needed. General movement speed improves rapidly in games that involve throwing and jumping. Full recoveries of 3 to 4 minutes are recommended in organized training sessions for both types of activities.

Because this is a most favorable age to improve flexibility, a range of suitable exercises should be performed as frequently as possible. It will allow children to become accustomed to flexibility exercises that are also helpful in the strengthening of ligaments and tendons. Games demanding twisting and dodging add to the development of flexibility and mobility.

As far as endurance is concerned, it should be kept in mind that the development of specific endurance (anaerobic capacity) is at this age restricted by physiological factors. It should take place in the following stages of training. A large volume of many-sided activities, including running games, skiing, ice skating and swimming are sufficient to develop general endurance in this stage.

Sprinting Technique

The learning of the sprinting technique in the introductory preparation stage concentrates on the development of relaxed running. Advanced techniques are left alone and introduced in the following basic stage. Emphasis should therefore be placed on the exploitation of the inherited coordination capacities to develop a natural running action. Only deviations from the most basic technique of sprinting should be corrected. This applies, in particular, to the movements deviating from the running direction and the placement of the feet.

Landing on the balls of the feet is one of the deciding facors in a correct technique. It reduces the breaking forces and allows for a fast driving action in a short contact with the track, thus increasing stride frequency and running speed. Children can achieve the correct placement of the feet only gradually, as their leg and ankle strength improves.

Practical experience has shown that the majority of children place their feet heel first until about the age of 12 when their strength level allows them to run on the balls of the feet. This process continues throughout the following basic training stage and care must be taken that children are not forced to run on the balls of the feet before their strength is sufficiently developed.

THE BASIC STAGE

This phase begins at the age of 11 to 12 and usually lasts two or three years. The main task is to strengthen physical capacities to establish a solid foundation for the future. While this takes place using a variety of sporting activities and games, young athletes are gradually guided towards their best suited event groups. They also learn the basic techniques of all track and field events.

A deciding factor in the choice of the event groups is the rate of the development of the physical capacities of the young athletes. The development rate is evaluated using reliable tests, observing particularly the improvements in speed and power capacities. An improvement around 9 to 10% in the first 18 months of this preparation stage is regarded as being good.

Physical Preparation

The development of the complex of physical capacities, employing a variety of exercises and sporting activities continues and follows generally the same pattern that was used in the introductory stage. However, participation in a large number of track and field events is added to the program, as jumping, throwing and hurdling are most helpful to develop power.

Strength is improved by a variety of exercises, emphasizing the most common weaknesses, namely the lack of strength in the abdominal, back and hamstring muscles. The shoulder girdle strength for girls should not be overlooked, nor the development of ankle and lower leg strength.

Strength training exercises that involve the use of additional resistances, in particular the barbell, should not be used. It is at this stage sufficient to concentrate on exercises against the athlete's own body weight, including jumping, apparatus gymnastics and acrobatics. The introduction to weight training takes place in the next preparation stage.

Games, particularly soccer, skiing and swimming are sufficient to develop general endurance. The inclusion of event specific endurance (anaerobic) is still not recommended training to the program, as this capacity is sufficiently developed in the large number of many-sided activities.

Sprinting Technique

Compared with the previous preparation stage, the improvement of sprinting technique is now based on more explanations and demonstrations. The learning is still based on the whole method, using mainly accelerations and runs at a controlled speed.

Attention is in the beginning directed to only one or two basic technique elements, such as the placement of the feet, movements in the running direction, an optimal driving action and relaxed running, without any tension in the shoulder and trunk muscles. Sprint specific exercises, such as high knee lift running, are used only sparingly. The same also applies to the learning of the starting technique and accelerations from the starting position. Both require a certain level of strength not yet available to young sprinters and must therefore be restricted to the establishment of only the most basic elements.

HOW TO PREDICT SPRINT POTENTIAL

by P. Siris, et al., USSR

The authors look at the performance dynamics of the world's best sprinters and offer interesting procedures for the prediction and selection of potential sprint talent.

The complex performance capacities of sprinters are made up from the anthropometric measurements (height, weight, proportion of limbs), the development levels of basic physical abilities (speed, speed oriented power) and their correlation with the biodynamical demands of sprinting (movement specific coordination).

Additional helpful information for the establishment of a model can be obtained from the development and performance dynamics of world's top sprinters. Looking first at the age of Olympic champions and finalists shows that it has stabilized around an average age of 25.3 years for men and 23.6 years for women in the 100m event. The corresponding average ages for the 200m are 25.7 and 23.8 years. These facts are useful in the choice of potential sprinters and the planning of training.

PERFORMANCE DYNAMICS

An analysis of the performance dynamics of the 37 world's best sprinters (average 100m time of 10.06 seconds) showed that all had an exceptionally fast initial performance (average 11.34 seconds). Most of them began specific training between the ages of 13 and 18 years. The athletes, who started specific training around 13 to 14 years, had an average initial time of 11.64 seconds, compared with an average first time of

11.15 seconds by those who started at an age of 17 to 18 years. Irrespective of when the specific training began, it took 8.2 to 9.4 years for the athletes to reach their top performance. Consequently the age of the top performance ranged from 22.2 to 27.8 years. (see Table 1.)

The intensity of the performance improvement depends on the sprinter's age and the level of initial preparation. However, irrespective of the age, the performance improves most rapidly during the first year of initial training. The athletes, who began specific training between the ages of 15 to 20 years, improved notably over the first four years, reaching their best times after seven or eight years. All age groups, irrespective of their initial performance and the rate of improvement had reached times 10.4 to 10.5 seconds in their fifth training year. Some, like Mennea, Wells, Leonard and others were capable of 10.0 to 10.1 seconds in their fourth or fifth training year.

The analysis showed further that top performances in sprinting are achieved only by athletes who had a rapid initial improvement rate, indicating that sprinting potential depends largely on genetic aspects. Table 2 gives some guidelines on the age range for the development of the performances.

Table 1: The performance dynamics of the world's best sprinters.

Specializing Age	Best 100m (sec.)	Age of Best Time (yrs.)	Years to Reach Best Time
13 - 14	10.05	22.2	9.3
15 - 16	10.11	22.9	8.2
17 - 18	10.10	24.8	8.3
19 - 20	10.00	27.8	9.4

Table 2: Age ranges in successful sprinting.

Distance (m)	First Success		Optimal Possibilities		Top Performances	
	Men	Women	Men	Women	Men	Women
100	19 - 21	17 - 19	22 - 24	20 - 22	25 - 26	23 - 25
200	19 - 21	17 - 19	22 - 24	20 - 22	25 - 26	23 - 25
400	22 - 23	20 - 21	24 - 26	22 - 24	27 - 28	25 - 26

Table 3: Anthropometric indicators at different performance levels (men).

Indicators	Performance Qualifications (sec.)				
	12.4 - 14.0	11.6 - 12.3	11.1 - 11.5	11.0 - 10.6	World's Best
Height (cm)	1.65 ± 1.67	1.77.7 ± 0.79	1.77.5 ± 1.39	1.79.2 ± 1.01	1.77.9 ± 0.83
Weight (kg)	52.1 ± 2.16	66.3 ± 1.09	68.8 ± 1.35	72.7 ± 0.96	76.2 ± 1.14
Index	315.76 ± 3.26	373.10 ± 3.23	387.60 ± 4.01	409.69 ± 5.16	428.33 ± 4.88

Table 4: The relative improvement of physical capacities of young sprinters (% compared with initial level).

Capacities	Training Years							
	0.5	1	1.5	2	2.5	3	3.5	4
Speed	2.8	4.8	5.3	5.8	6.5	8.6	6.4	7.7
Power	2.4	5.4	10.8	12.8	17.9	17.6	14.1	20.1
Strength	14.2	17.7	26.5	31.3	37.9	37.9	50.1	52.5
Endurance	9.1	11.2	14.0	15.5	16.7	16.7	18.8	20.1

PHYSICAL CAPACITIES

Contrary to many other track and field events, the anthropometric measurements have no great importance in sprinting. Top performances have been achieved by tall as well as short athletes. However, there is some correlation between the height-weight index of an athlete and the sprint performance, which can be used as a guide (see Table 3).

The development of physical capacities has an important place in sprint training, as good performances depend on speed, strength, power and specific endurance. The selection of potential sprinters is usually based on testing these capacities. However, coaching experience has shown that athletes with the best test results are often exceeded by those with poor results after two or three years.

This occurs because the tests are used to evaluate children who differ considerably in their rate of development. Consequently there is little value in predicting sprinting potential on a single series of tests. Sprinting ability predictions are far more reliable when they are based on the rate of development during training processes. The authors, following the development of 23 young sprinters in the 13 to 17 age range over four years, discovered that their uneven development of physical capacities showed the fastest improvement rate during the first 18 months of specific training. The improvements took place in the following order: speed, endurance, strength and power (see Table 4).

It was further discovered that the initial evaluation of potential sprint talent turned out to be correct after four years of training in only a few cases. We discovered also that the most reliable test indicators were the vertical jump and the index of combined jumping power, while the standing long jump and the 20m from a flying start appeared to have limited value. The 30m and 60m sprints from a crouch start and the initial 100m time had also limited correlation with the 100m end result.

Experiments showed that using the initial physical performance tests as a guide would result in an 82% of failure in the prediction of potential sprint talent. The failure rate would be reduced to 75% when the prediction is based on the initial

100m time. It would be reduced further to only 21% when the prediction takes into consideration the 100m time improvement over the first 18 months of specific training and to 11% when based on the improvement rate of the physical performance capacities over the first 18 months of training.

PREDICTIONS

The experiment allowed the authors to establish a formula for the prediction of potential capacities of sprinters, based on the initial level of the capacities and their rate of development over the first 18 months:

$$W = \frac{100 \times (V2 - V1)}{0.5 \times (V1 + V2)} \%$$

W = Development rate, V1 = initial test results, V2 = final test results.

In general, the following can be applied:

❏ A high level of initial physical capacities and
  • rapid rate of development—excellent (9.9 to 10.1 seconds)
  • medium rate of development—good (10.2 to 10.4 seconds)
  • poor rate of development—average (10.5 to 10.7 seconds)
❏ A medium level of initial physical capacities and
  • rapid rate of development—good (10.2 to 10.4 seconds)
  • medium rate of development—average (10.5 to 10.7 seconds)
  • poor rate of development—poor (11.0 to 11.3 seconds)
❏ A low level of initial physical capacities and
  • rapid rate of development—average (10.6 to 10.9 seconds)

Available information and practical experience makes it possible to present some guidelines to evaluate the rate of improvement of young sprinters in the 13 to 14½ age range. These guidelines (see Table 5) are reasonably reliable for the prediction of potential talent.

SPECIFIC CHARACTERISTICS

Top sprinters possess an excellent movement rhythm, have a fast driving action and a relatively long flight phase. V. Balsevic of the Soviet Union has established that untrained youngsters perform their driving phase in 150 to 160 m/sec. (milli-seconds) compared to 110 to 130 m/sec. by average athletes. There are, of course, some youngsters with an 80 to 90 m/sec. driving phase. They are excellent sprint prospects. Table 6 presents some recommended times to evaluate the driving phase.

Table 6: Average length of the driving phase for young sprinters

Age	Driving Phase in m/sec.		
	Excellent	Good	Average
13	110	115	120
14	108	112	118
15	105	110	115
16	103	108	112
17	102	106	110

It should be finally noted that there are morphological differences in the suitability for one or another sprint distance. Sprinters, who are successful in the 100m and only average in the 200m are usually medium height (174cm) and weight (73.2kg). The best 200m runners, in contrast, are on an average taller (182.0cm) and lighter

Table 5: Initial levels and improvement rates of 13 to 14 ½-year-old sprinters during the first 18 months of training.

Test	Initial Level			Improvement Rate (%)		
	High (& better)	Average	Poor (& below)	High (& better)	Average	Poor (& below)
20m flying start (sec.)	2.1	2.4 ± 0.36	2.7	12.5	8.2 ± 2.16	3.9
30m crouch start (sec.)	4.1	4.4 ± 0.38	4.8	10.0	5.1 ± 2.4	0.5
60m crouch start (sec.)	7.7	8.3 ± 0.31	8.9	7.9	4.5 ± 1.7	1.1
100m crouch start (sec.)	12.2	13.5 ± 0.62	14.7	8.0	5.2 ± 1.4	2.4
St. long jump (cm)	265	233 ± 9.3	214	9.0	6.2 ± 1.4	3.4
Vertical jump (cm)	60	53.2 ± 3.06	47	11.8	7.6 ± 2.1	3.4
600m run (sec.)	116.4	119.1 ± 8.35	135.3	15.9	15.1 ± 1.9	11.3
Dynamometric strength (kg)	140.0	109.4 ± 15.8	78.0	30.4	23.2 ± 3.6	19.6

Italy's Pietro Mennea, shown here victorious at the 1974 European Championships 200m, was one of the sprinters cited by the author who achieved times of 10.4 or 10.5 by their fifth training year.

(71.8kg). The height-weight indexes for top 100m sprinters average 419.7 g/cm, compared with 392 g/cm for the best 200m exponents.

Taller sprinters cover the distance with longer strides and less stride frequency than shorter ahtletes. They take around 44 to 46 strides for the 100m and are usually performing well in the 200 and 400m races. Shorter sprinters, on the other hand, take 48 to 53 strides for the 100m and are generally capable for exploiting their work capacity mainly over short distances (60 to 100m).

As speed losses occur in the 200m mainly through stride frequency, while the stride length remains virtually unchanged, the taller athletes have an advantage. Shorter athletes, depending mainly on stride frequency, tire faster and have to exploit their speed endurance in order to succeed in the 200m.

SPRINTING TECHNIQUE IN THE BASIC TRAINING PHASE

by Dr. K. Erdman, German Democratic Republic

The author stresses the importance of establishing the essential aspects of sprint technique, particularly the running action on the balls of the feet, in the early stages of basic training.

Faults in sprint technique because of a high level of automation can turn into factors that restrict performance. Essential aspects of technique should therefore be observed early in the basic training phase, when an appropriate sprint technique must be learned and performed at maximal speed.

The running stride is usually divided (see Figure 1) into the following phases:

- the rear swinging phase (1), that allows relaxation and makes preparations for the knee lift;
- the front swinging phase (2), that influences the stride length and the preparation for the landing;
- the front support phase (3), during which the breaking effect should be kept as restricted as possible;
- the rear support phase (4), that decides the force and the direction of the drive and with it the forward motion.

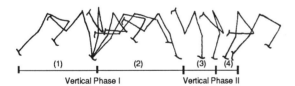

Figure 1: The structure of the running stride

The technical mastery of the movements at maximal speed that corresponds to the accepted technical model is the basic requirement for high level performances in sprinting events. The ability to achieve this mastery depends, in particular, on an effective exploitation of the driving forces responsible for horizontal velocity in the rear support phase and the reduction of the breaking forces in the front support phase. The essential key factor in the sprinting technique is therefore the placement of the foot in the support phase.

TECHNIQUE ESSENTIALS

Studies in the 9 to 12 years age range show a variety of foot placements among the young athletes. While the placement on the ball of the foot is predominant among the better 12-year-olds, the 9-year-olds are using several variations of foot placements. There are, next to a clear heel first placement, those who land on the full foot, on the outer edge of the foot and also those who employ a different foot placement for the right and left leg.

Why is it necessary to concentrate on running on the ball of the foot early in technique development in the basic training phase? The explanation is in the duration of the support phase and its correlation with the maximum speed, established from high speed films (200 frames a second). The results showed the following:

1. It was possible to establish a correlation between the support phase and the maximum speed. As maximum speed represents the main task, the aim should be to achieve the shortest possible support phase.

2. A correct placement on the ball of the foot makes it possible to shorten the support phase and consequently to increase speed. Our film observations showed that the quality of the foot placement was decisive for the duration of the support times. A technically correct execution of a sprinting stride has therefore a positive influence on speed performances.

3. A heel-first foot placement, with a relatively long support phase and limited speed, is responsible for reduced speed and should consequently be avoided.

4. Differences between the support phases of the right and the left foot occurred because of the

different qualities of the foot placements. The cause for this appeared to be that the stronger leg differed from the other in duration of the support phase.

In summary, the results show the following:

- The technical factor that most significantly influences performance in the speed complex is characterized by the duration of the support phase of the foot placement. Short support phases are the sign of a high speed performance.
- Based on the above, it is important to achieve and to establish at maximum speed a technically correct on the ball foot placement on both sides.

Technically correct sprinting means a performance with an actively reaching foot placement. The aim to achieve the highest possible speed depends on the establishment of an optimal ratio of the stride length (l) and stride frequency (f) — $v = l \times f$. Landing on the ball of the foot makes it possible to reduce the breaking forces in the front support phase and therefore assist the frequency of the movements.

The aim in the rear support phase (driving phase) is the optimal exploitation of the driving forces (level and direction) to develop horizontal speed. It is reflected in an energetic stretching drive and pre-tension of the muscles in the front support phase.

DEVELOPMENT GUIDELINES

Therefore, the following methodical procedures have to be observed in the technique development of young athletes:

- a "whole" learning approach (the ABC's of sprinting)
- combining the technique development with specific physical conditioning (particularly the strengthening of the leg muscles) methods
- a conscious concentration on single movement elements (running on the balls of the feet!)
- the most important basic exercises: acceleration and tempo runs
- a continuous use of the sprint ABC's to improve technical elements
- a gradual increase of speed, as well as lengthening the distances, to allow for the most effective controllable speed (sub-maximal) for technical perfection.

These basic guidelines are applied to the training procedures with specific emphasis on running on the balls of the feet. It is essential in the schooling of the sprint technique to create awareness of the correct movement performance. Charts and picture sequences allow the young athletes to recognize a technically correct foot placement (straight and on the ball of the foot), as well as faulty techniques.

In turn, this requires from the coach a good technical knowledge of sprinting and the ability to convert this knowledge into a methodical approach. Theory lessons presented early in the basic training phase, allow in the presentation of "correct" versus "incorrect" to improve learning processes and to create awareness of certain main points of the technique.

Attention in the actual training should regularly be given to running on the balls of the feet. Advice, such as "run softly", "drive from the ball of the foot", make yourself tall" are helpful. Running on the ball of the foot is the most significant characteristic of a good sprinting performance. It is therefore important to stress the methodical development of this action as early as possible under competitive conditions.

TRAINING OF YOUNG SPRINTERS

by B. Tabatshnik and B. Timoschenko, USSR

The authors discuss the training of young sprinters, employing a program with an amazing variety of physical activities, emphasizing jumping exercises and relatively little actual sprinting.

The first two training years of young athletes lead to the initial specialization stage. The main aim during these years is to assure many-sided development and an improvement of general physical capacities. However, the development of speed capacities through maximum speed runs under standard conditions should not be overemphasized. Far more effective is the use of uphill runs, upstairs runs, runs in the sand and runs with a weighted vest, alternated with runs under normal conditions.

At this stage it is also time to begin the learning of the basic elements of the sprint relay, while variety in training is achieved by games (basketball, soccer, handball, etc.) that demand continual changes in running speed under different conditions. It should be kept in mind that this is an excellent age for the development of movement speed, but the development of movement abilities must be preceded by improvement of physical capacities.

For this reason there is no need to rush into the learning of the crouch start. In the beginning children should learn the standing start and accelerations from a variety of positions, responding to different commands. For example, starting from walking or jogging, starting from a position with the hands supported 20 to 30cm above the track level, starting with one arm support, etc.

Strength and power at this stage are developed by bounding exercises, standing jumps, exercises with medicine balls and resistance exercises (50 to 80% of the athlete's body weight).

There must also be a lot of variety in the competition program. Athletes at this stage are advised to take part in long and triple jumps, hurdles, high jump, shot or medicine ball put, 30 and 60m sprints, as well as 150, 200 and 300m runs and relays.

It is advisable to employ regular control tests to check the development of young sprinters. A suggested test battery for the second training year with recommended norms is shown in Table 1.

Table 1: Control tests and norms for the second training year in sprinting.

TEST	NORMS	
	BOYS	**GIRLS**
60m (sec)	7.6 - 7.4	8.1 - 7.9
100m (sec)	11.8 - 11.6	13.0 - 12.8
200m (sec)	24.5 - 23.8	27.0 - 26.5
30m flying (sec)	3.3 - 3.2	3.6 - 3.4
30m crouch (sec)	4.3 - 4.2	4.6 - 4.5
150m (sec)	19.0 - 18.0	21.5 - 20.0
300m (sec)	40.0 - 39.0	45.0 - 44.0
St. long jump (cm)	250 - 265	220 - 240
St. triple jump (cm)	740 - 780	640 - 680
St. 10 hops (m)	25 - 27	22 - 24

TRAINING SUGGESTIONS

The following examples of training microcycles (weeks) are selected from various periods in the yearly plan and include work performed in the first and second preparation, competition and training camps periods.

Microcycles

Preparation Period (General I)
Day 1: Warm-up (7 to 8 minutes jogging, 12 to 15 minutes exercises). Shot throws (3 to 4kg) upward-forward and backward-overhead. Running technique 9 x 30 to 40m. Accelerations 3 x 60 to 80m. Partner exercises for the development of back, abdominal and leg strength. Bounding 5 x 30m. Jogging 4 to 5 minutes.

Day 2: Warm-up. Medicine ball exercises (80 throws). Flexibility exercises (10 minutes). Uphill running 6-8 x 50 to 60m. Soccer or basketball (40 minutes). Vertical jumps (20 reps). Relaxed running on a soft surface 2 x 150 to 200m. Jogging 4 to 5 minutes.

Day 3: Warm-up. Running with a 4kg weight vest 8 x 40m. Accelerations 3 x 60 to 80m. Standing jumps (15 reps). Basic hurdles exercises. Varied speed runs 8-10 x 200m (80m fast + 120m relaxed). Jogging 4 x 5 minutes.

Day 4: Rest.

Day 5: Warm-up. Medicine ball exercises 5-6 x 10 to 15 reps. Running technique 6 x 40m. Accelerations 3 x 60m. Uphill running 5 x 100m. Bounding 5 x 40m. Jogging 4 to 5 minutes.

Day 6: Warm-up. General gymnastics with a partner (10 to 12 minutes). Basketball or soccer (50 minutes).

Day 7: Rest.

Preparation Period (General II)
Day 1: Warm-up. Running technique 6 x 40m. Accelerations 3 x 80m. Upward jumps from 3 to 4 strides, aiming for an object (20 reps). Abdominal exercises 2-3 x 8 to 10 reps. Specific hurdles exercises. Games (2 x 20 minutes). Jogging 4 to 5 minutes.

Day 2: Warm-up. Medicine ball throws (60 to 80 reps). Running technique 4 x 40m. Accelerations 3 to 60m. Starts from different positions, walking, jogging, leaning, etc. (20 reps). Jumps over 5 to 7 hurdles (10 reps). Relaxed runs 2 x 120m. Flexibility exercises. Jogging 4 to 5 minutes.

Day 3: Warm-up. Shot throws forward-upward (7 reps), backward over the head (7 reps). Runs with a weight vest (2 to 3kg) 6 x 40m. Long jumps from a 7 to 9 stride run-up (10 reps). Repetition runs with 85 to 90% intensity 180m +150m + 120m. Jogging 4 to 5 minutes.

Day 4: Rest.

Day 5: Warm-up. Standing long jumps (5 reps). Exercises with the barbell (press, clean, squat, split jumps), 2 x 8 to 10 reps. Knees to chest jumps 4 x 15 to 20 reps. Flexibility exercises. Jogging 4 to 5 minutes.

Day 6: Warm-up. Basketball (30 minutes). Cross country run (20 minutes).

Day 7: Rest.

Preparation Period (Specific I)
Day 1: Warm-up. Shot throws upward-forward (3 to 4kg). Accelerations with a weight vest (2 to 3kg) 3 x 60 to 80m. Starts from different positions (15 reps). Take-offs every 3rd, 4th and 5th stride 4 x 40 to 50m. Standing jumps (20 to 25 reps). Jogging 4 to 5 minutes.

Day 2: Warm-up. Standing long jumps (10 reps), standing triple jumps (10 reps). Crouch starts 12 x 20m. Varied speed runs 3-4 x 120m (40m fast + 20m relaxed, etc.). Jogging 4 to 5 minutes.

Day 3: Warm-up. Basketball (15 mintues). General exercises (10 to 12 minutes). Running technique 6 x 40m. Specific hurdles exercises (5 to 7 minutes). Hurdling over three hurdles (76.2cm) 5-6 x 80m (9 to 11 strides between the hurdles). Medicine ball throws (100 to 120 reps). Varied speed runs 6-10 x 200m (80m fast, 120m relaxed). Jogging 4 to 5 minutes.

Day 4: Swimming (30 to 45 minutes).

Day 5: Warm-up. Standing long jumps (8 reps), standing triple jumps (5 reps), long jumps from a 6 to 12 stride run-up (6 to 8 reps). Barbell exercises (press, clean, jumps from a squat, step-ups) 2 x 8 to 10 reps of each (25 to 40kg). Jogging 4 to 5 minutes.

Day 6: Outdoor games, skiing, skating, etc. Sauna.

Day 7: Rest.

Preparation Period (Specific II)
Day 1: Warm-up. Medicine ball throws (50 reps). Running technique 6 x 60m. Hurdling 6-8 x over four hurdles (76 to 84cm) with 7, 5 and 3 strides in between the hurdles (placed 12 to 13m to the 1st, followed by 16 to 18m, 12 to 13m and 8 to 9m in between the hurdles). Varied speed runs 3-4 x 120m (40m fast + 10 to 12 strides relaxed). Jogging 4 to 5 minutes.

Day 2: Warm-up. Standing long jumps (10 reps), standing triple jumps (5 reps). Accelerations 3 x 30 to 40m. Crouch starts 10 x 20m. Uphill runs (3 to 4°) 2 x 60m, followed by 2 x 60m on the flat, etc. (3 series). Jogging 4 to 5 minutes.

Day 3: Warm-up. Games (15 minutes). General

exercises (10 to 12 minutes). Shot throws (10 reps). Take-offs every 5th and 7th stride 3 x 60m each leg. Runs with 85 to 90% intensity 150 + 120 + 80m (6 to 8 minute recoveries). Bounding 3 x 30m. Jogging 4 to 5 minutes.

Day 4: Rest.

Day 5: Warm-up. Downhill runs 6 x 30m. Accelerations (downhill) 4 x 60m. Crouch starts 6-8 x 20m. Relay running (3 to 5 changeovers). Squat jumps 3-4 x 25 to 30 reps. Jogging 4 to 5 minutes.

Day 6: Warm-up. Games (15 minutes). Barbell exercises 4 to 5 exercises (2 series, 8 to 10 reps). Games (20 to 30 minutes).

Day 7: Rest.

Training Camps
Day 1: A.M.—Exercises on gymnastics apparatus. Accelerations 5-6 x 40m. Uphill accelerations (4 to 5°) 4-5 x 50 to 60m. Upward jumps, aiming for objectives (20 reps). P.M.—Games.

Day 2: A.M.—General partner exercises. Flexibility exercises. Specific hurdles exercises (technique). Games (20 to 30 minutes). Relay practice. P.M.—Swimming.

Day 2: A.M.—General partner exercises. Flexibility exercises. Specific hurdles exercises (technique). Games (20 to 30 minutes). Relay practice. P.M.—Swimming.

Day 3: A.M.—General gymnastics with acrobatic elements. Throwing of stones or balls. Varied speed runs 8-10 x 200 to 250m (60 to 80m fast, 120 to 150m relaxed). P.M.—Warm-up. High jump training. Uphill runs 3-4 x 60m.

Day 4: A.M.—20 to 25 minutes cross country running. Throwing of stones or balls. P.M.—Basketball or soccer.

Day 5: A.M.—General exercises (12 to 15 minutes). Resistance exercises, flexibility exercises. Handball (30 minutes). P.M.—Swimming.

Day 6: A.M.—General partners exercises. Standing long jumps (15). Relay practice. Games.

Day 7: Hiking (10 to 12km). Games. Swimming.

Competition Period
   Usually three days of training with one or two days set aside for competitions. The content of the training is similar to days 1, 2 and 5 in Preparation Period (Specific II).

PREPARATION OF JUNIOR FEMALE 400M RUNNERS

by V.A. Fedorets, USSR

A long term development plan of young potential female 400m talent from the age of 8 years to their peak preparation stage between 21 and 23 years. The five-stage plan is designed to avoid exhausting the central nervous system and keep the dropout rate to a minimum.

Many years of systematic training is of immense importance in the development of girls in the sprinting events. It enables to take the most talented athletes to the top in a planned way with minimal dropouts. The long term training of women sprinters therefore has to be designed taking into consideration the laws of biological development and the data on physiology, psychology and pedagogy.

The foundation of such a program is to establish annual increases in the results over the basic distances of 60, 100, 200 and 400m. The annual individual improvements in performances has the following pattern:

- 8 to 12 years of age: an even development of results as speed depends largely on the development of nervous processes
- 12 to 16 years of age: a heterochronized improvement of results because of sexual maturation
- 16 years and over: a synchronized improvement of results through the development of physical performance capacities.

Thus, to prepare athletes for international level we use five developmental stages, each of which contains its own specific objectives.

STAGE 1: LEARNING
(12 to 14 years)

The objective of the learning processes are to establish a structure of movement for the sprint and the development of the required motor habits, coordination of flexibility. An acquaintance with closely related events, the long jump and the hurdles, also takes place.

The methods used in this period consist of play training and exercises for an all-round development, such as acrobatics, gymnastics, team games, running exercises within the 70 to 80% intensity range and intermittent cross country running in the woods. In addition, a number of technical exercises for the development of fast running technique and the basic sprint start are also included.

STAGE 2: THE BASE
(15 to 16 years)

The task here is to lay a foundation for the functional performance capacities of the organism and physical strength for the future specific sprint training. At the same time the development of the starting technique is continued.

The volume of training is increased in this stage through the length and the number of distances within the 70 to 80% range of the maximal. Only in the competitive season is the intensity increased to 90 to 95%. Light weights, 40 to 50% of the athlete's own body weight, are now employed in an attempt to strengthen musculature and ligaments. Jumping exercises to improve power also are employed.

Another aspect of this period is the introduction of varied speed runs and specific preparatory running exercises. We use varied speed runs and sprints over short distances in a small volume with an intensity of 80 to 90% . Attention is paid to the position of the body, the arm action and the placement of the feet.

STAGE 3: SPECIALIZED PREPARATION
(17 to 18 years)

The aim at this stage is to stabilize the motor habits of sprinting at speed and the acceleration from the start. Training in the range of special work now reaches 60 to 70% of the top national and international sprinters. The volume of functional and technical training approaches 80 to 90% of that of adult athletes.

We continue to improve the technique of running at speed and the start and at this stage increase the total volume of work with weights, which constitutes 60 to 70% of the weight training of adult athletes. The maximum weights lifted also are increased.

In the main the same methods are used as in Stage 2, but the range is narrower. There is less gymnastics and acrobatics, more attention is paid to the long jump and the high jump, and team games are employed for active restoration.

STAGE 4: IMPROVEMENT
(19 to 20 years)

The task here is to create stability in the athlete's physical and functional capacities. Increased speeds are used for the development of the start and sprinting speed.

Besides physical and technical tasks being tackled at this stage, there are a number of circumstances to overcome with athletes who could leave the sport, as many indeed do. The coach working with junior girls must therefore know all about the female physiology and female psychology. The coach has to be single-minded and prove to the athlete that she should strive in life for the goal that will enable her to understand herself and the world. In a word, the coach should be a diplomat capable of convincing the young athletes.

As far as the physical load is concerned, the total volume of speed work is increased with an intensity in the 90 to 95% range in specific training stages. At the same time up to 5 or 6km a week is covered in 100 to 300m sections with 75 to 85% intensity.

The work with weights should reach 4 to 5 tons and includes exercises with 40 to 60 repetitions performed against the athlete's own body weight for each chosen muscle group. In addition, the athlete covers 25 to 30km a week in cross country running during the preparation period, subsequently changing to speed running in restricted volumes.

Most important at this stage is not to exhaust the nervous system.

STAGE 5: PEAK PREPARATION
(21 to 23 years)

The paramount task at this stage is to nurture the athlete's sprinting capacities to an absolute maximum. This includes speed, power and speed endurance and a high level of skill in order to reach international level performance. The range of training means at this level becomes relatively narrower with increased intensities.

The volume of running distances up to 100m at an intensity of 91 to 95% is increased considerably, as is other resistance running, such as using weight vests, lead belts and uphill sprinting. The volume of distances over 100m with an intensity of 80 to 90% also is increased. We begin to give at this stage priority to fast cross country tempo runs over normal cross country runs. For example, 500m + 500m, 1km + 1km, 2km + 2km and so on.

A great deal of attention at this stage is given to the development of absolute strength of an athlete to establish a base for the development of power capacities. This takes place by using fast weight training exercises against 30 to 40% resistances at the maximum and various jumping exercises, combined in sets of power development. An example of such a set is:

1. Lifting of a 30kg barbell five times as fast as possible.
2. Five squats with a 50kg weight as fast as possible.
3. Jumps over 76cm high hurdles in a fast succession.
4. Fast bounding over 30m.
5. Maximum speed sprint over 30m.

We also pay attention to the development of strength endurance, which assists, in turn, the strengthening of muscles and ligaments. This is particularly important during injuries to the support apparatus, as the work may partially replace running, while the functional stage of the organism is still maintained. The work is performed with weights 40 to 60% of the athlete's body weight with a maximal number of repetitions. Another method involves using a set of 8 to 12 exercises against limited resistances (10 to 20kg) in the following regime:

30 seconds work, 30 seconds recovery, 1 minute work, 1 minute recovery, 2 minutes work, 1 minute recovery, etc. This may take 5 to 15 minutes of pure work.

An example of a set with 20kg weights is as follows:
1. Regular barbell press (30 seconds or 1 minute)
2. Press behind the neck
3. Bent-over rowing

4. Forward bend-over
5. Abdominal exercise
6. Leg raise
7. Hip extension
8. Foot muscle exercise.

Each set is completed with 2 to 3 repetitions of a 30m sprint at 80 to 85% intensity.

Despite the fact that training is getting harder in this stage, it should not be monotonous. An employment of a limited range of training means leads to a stabilization of the stride frequency and stride length. It may thereby hamper progress in speed development and lead to regression. Consequently, to reach a given objective and to develop a particular capacity requires a wise selection of training methods and their variations. Varying methods also enable the athlete to extend the preparation stage of her training and subsequently makes it possible to also extend the competition stage.

In order to maintain a particular quality in the competitive stage methods should be varied to stimulate the organism with small, but accentuated dosages, without exhausting the central nervous system, which, after all is the sprinter's main motor.

**Grit Breuer, GDR,
1988 World Junior 400m Champion**

CHAPTER V:
SPRINT RELAY

RELAY TECHNIQUE

by Dr. Gerd Schroter, German Democratic Republic

Although there are considerable differences in the length of track and field coaches training courses from nation to nation, the basic event-specific material appears to have little variations, as can be seen from the following article on relay running.

BASIC FACTORS

The performance capacity in relays depends, above all, on
- the sprinting ability of the team members and
- the perfection of the changeover proceedings.

Other factors that influence the performance include:
- certain tactical questions in the running order of the team, as well as
- an understanding of the team members about their collective responsibility in the competition.

The changeover, besides the above mentioned factors, depends significantly on the quality of the established technique, including:
- an appropriate utilization of the changeover zone,
- the type of the changeover,
- the decisive elements of a precise acceleration of the outgoing runner, as well as
- the technique of the changeover.

A specific aim in the relays is for the outgoing runner to accumulate speed before the baton is handed over, so that the changeover occurs "fluently." The higher the running speed at the moment of the baton exchange, the more effective is the changeover. All efforts to improve the changeover technique are therefore directed to avoid, within the necessary safety, as much as possible a drop in the baton speed. This can be achieved, above all, when:
- the incoming runner, in spite of preparations for the baton change, can maintain the running speed;
- the outgoing runner has already reached a high speed before the changeover.

THE CHANGEOVER

Utilization of the Zone

According to the competition rules the changeover must take place in a 20m zone. The outgoing runner is allowed to start another 10m further back (Fig. 1). In order to have the longest possible acceleration distance at the disposal of the outgoing runner, the changeover should take place in the second half of the zone. Excellent changeovers therefore occur close to the end line of the zone.

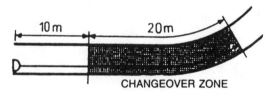

Figure 1: The changover zone.

A necessary safety allowance is, as a rule, included in the changeover proceedings to avoid disqualification. An optimum would be (Fig. 2):
- allowance for a 17 to 20m long acceleration distance prior to the changeover,
- completion of the changeover approximately in the last third of the zone.

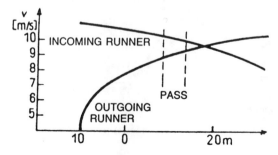

Figure 2: The profile of velocities in the changeover zone.

Table 1: Customary changeover types.

	Outside	Inside	Combined
Incoming runner			
— Baton carrying hand	left	right	combined
— Running path in the zone	outside	inside	1st and 3rd = inside change
Outgoing runner			
— Baton taking hand	right	left	2nd change= outside change
— Running path in the zone	inside	outside	
— Necessary change of hand	right to left	left to right	not needed

Types of changeovers

There are no major performance influencing differences between the three customary types of changeovers: outside-inside-combination (Table 1). However, considering the advantages and disadvantages of:
- the safety factors of the changeover,
- the path of the runners in the changeover zone (particularly in the curve), and
- tactical calculations (replacement runners), leads to the preference of the outside change.

Procedures

An efficient changeover is not only recognizable visually, but above all measurable by the time required for the baton to cover the changeover zone. This, next to the sprint capacity, depends on the appropriate procedures of the changeover, in particular on:
- a suitably established check mark and an efficient starting position that decides a correctly timed and powerful start of the outgoing runner,
- a maximal acceleration of the outgoing runner without being influenced by the forthcoming passing action, as well as the maintenance of the speed of the incoming runner, and
- the fastest possible, but safe passing of the baton.

Check mark

A check mark signifies the spot where the outgoing runner starts when the mark is reached by the incoming runner. The distance of the mark from the end line of the zone is established individually, taking into consideration:
- the running speed of the incoming runner, and
- the reaction and acceleration capacity of the outgoing runner.

The following applies as a general guide:
Men: 7.00 - 9.00m
Women: 6.50 - 7.00m
Children: 5.00 - 6.00m.

The exact check mark is established by experimenting in training. However, competition atmosphere, current form and other similar factors could require adjustments to the check mark.

Equally important to the precise establishment of the check mark is the exact start of the outgoing runner. It is relatively difficult for the outgoing runner with a restricted angle of vision to catch the exact moment the incoming runner reaches the check mark. Even experienced sprinters, under the emotional strain of the race, make mistakes.

Starting positions

The starting position of the outgoing runner must allow for:
- favorable conditions for an explosive start and a fast acceleration,
- a good observation of the approaching incoming runner.

The start occurs from a standing start position in the 10m acceleration zone. It should provide the best possible prerequisites for acceleration (Fig. 3).

Figure 3: Possible starting positions for the outgoing runner.

The legs are placed apart with the toes pointing forward. As the incoming runner approaches the knees are flexed, the weight is shifted on the balls of the feet and the trunk is bent. The arms are placed in the running direction, diagonally to the legs. The twist of the body for the necessary observation of the incoming runner should be as small as possible. The outgoing runner should only move the head, according to the type of the changeover, to one side over the shoulder or under the front arm to look back.

A position with one hand supported on the track is also possible.

Acceleration

The outgoing runner must direct all effort into reaching the highest possible rate of acceleration as soon as the incoming runner has reached the check mark. This requires:

- extreme concentration,
- maximum reaction and a fast start, as well as
- maximum acceleration.

The acceleration in relay running must be similar to that in normal sprinting, unrestricted by the task of the baton pass that follows. Looking back, or extending the arm back too early, leads to speed losses. The running track, according to the type of the changeover, must be kept close to the inside or the outside of the lane, to avoid impeding the incoming runner.

The incoming runner must in this phase attempt to maintain the speed. The normal running rhythm continues with the arm movements still active. An early forward movement of the baton and a trunk lean will lead to speed losses.

Passing

The technique of passing aims to:
- pass the baton safely,
- perform the pass while disturbing the running rhythm as little as possible.

The passing action should therefore be limited to two or three running strides. It begins when the incoming runner is 1.5 to 2m from the partner and gives an acoustic signal to extend a relaxed arm backward.

The outgoing runner, without changing a frontal sprint position, is expected to extend the arm with a steady hand backward to provide an easy target for the baton. Only then will the incoming runner reach forward with the baton carrying hand to complete the changeover.

There are two major passing techniques:
- the upward technique, in which the receiving hand is placed facing down with a wide angle between the thumb and the rest of the fingers. The incoming runner passes the baton with an upward movement (Fig. 4a).
- the downward technique, in which the hand is placed with its back facing down. The incoming runner passes the baton with a downward movement (Fig. 4b)

Table 2: An overview of the structure of the changeover procedures.

PHASES		
PREPARATION	**ACCELERATION**	**PASSING**
From—establishment of the check mark To—start	—start —2-3m between the runners	—2-3m between the runners —completed pass
FUNCTIONS		
Establishment of prerequisites for an exact start, speed and safe passing	Maintenance (incoming) and development (outgoing) of speed as the runners approach.	Fast and secure passing of the baton at the best possible speed.
CHARACTERISTICS		
Incoming runner: —maximal speed —short running path (inside the lane in the curve) —baton in the correct hand	—maintenance of speed —approach on the correct side of the lane —maintenance of proper sprint action	—correctly timed signal —safe placement of the baton in the hand of outgoing runner. —remaining in the lane until the pass has been completed.
Outgoing runner: —correct placement of check mark —correct starting position: • on the correct side of the lane • deep driving position • favorable view of incoming runner • concentration	—exactly timed start —maximal acceleration • fast reaction • high stride frequency • frontal running position • full arm action	—extension of the arm with: • correct hand position • nearly straight arm • hand held steady —maintenance of running speed —change of the baton to the other hand (if required).

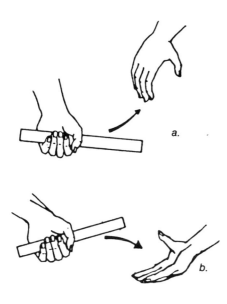

If inside or outside types of changeover are used, the outgoing runner must shift the baton immediately into the other hand.

SUMMARY

The main criterion of an effective changeover is to transport the baton in the *shortest time* possible inside the available changeover zone with optimal safety. An overview of the structure of this is presented in Table 2.

Figure 4: Major passing techniques.

Table 2: Stick figure sequence.

PREPARATION OF SPRINT RELAY TEAMS

by J. N. Zhubryakov, USSR

The Soviet Union's 4 x 100m men's relay teams have had success down through the years despite normally having only mediocre individual sprinters. The USSR men's 4 x 100 team has won two of the last three Olympic gold medals (1980 and 1988). The author lays out a year's training program, showing how thoroughly a relay team can approach the task to meet the challenge of international competitions.

The men's and women's 4 x 100m relays are an integral part of the track and field program in all competitions, including the Olympic Games and World Championships. Of all the relays the 4 x 100m is the most complex, due to many factors. The main one of these is to obtain high level stable results from athletes, who must not only have excellent speed capacities but also must be capable of passing the baton at high speed.

It is well known that teams consisting of sprinters with excellent individual performances over the 100m can be responsible for slower results than quartets with lower individual times. Consequently, the final result in a 4 x 100m relay depends not only on the speed potential of the sprinters, but to a large extent on the technique of interaction between the runners in passing the baton within the 20m changeover zone.

The principal work in this direction must be executed in the pre-season preparation period. A cycle of 5 to 6 weeks is sufficient here to establish stable motor habits for the changeover. The interaction and speed capacities are improved in the main part of a training session, consisting of not less than 420m (120m for receiving and 300m for passing) of high intensity (97 to 100%) running in a single workout. The number of baton exchanges takes place 8 to 10 times.

The starting and running techniques in the relay are basically the same as in normal 100 and 200m sprints. The distinguishing feature is that the first runner holds the baton in the right hand and runs on the inside of the lane, the second runner takes the baton in the left hand and runs closer to the outside of the lane, the third runner takes the baton in the right hand and runs close to the inside of the lane before passing it to the final runner. The last three legs have the right to start 10m outside the changeover zone and the actual transfer must take place in the second half of the changeover zone (usually 2 to 3 strides before the end line. This means that the outgoing runner has 25 to 26m to accelerate.

PRINCIPLES

In order to select athletes for the different relay legs it is sensible to find out their capacities for a particular section (the second and third runner cover longer disances). In the aim to produce best relay results it also is advisable to establish each athlete's full potential for running sections on the straight and around the bend.

These individuals' abilities must be taken into account in deciding the running order of a relay team, considering the following:

First leg—priority goes to an athlete who has a good start, can run the bend and pass the baton well.

Second leg—the choice goes to an athlete who is confident in receiving and passing the baton, runs well in the straight and possesses sufficient speed endurance.

Third leg—the selection goes to the sprinter who is confident and reliable in receiving and passing the baton, can run the bend well and possess sufficient speed endurance.

Fourth leg—here we normally select a runner who receives the baton well, is efficient in running the straight and has a high degree of competitive spirit.

There are several methods of baton passing. The Soviet national team uses the alternate hand upsweep method. In this method the athlete receives the baton with the arm fully extended, or slightly bent in the elbow. The hand is not inverted but is taken back with the wrist held down. In this open downward position the thumb forms an angle with the fingers into which the baton is inserted by an upward swing of the incoming runner. At the moment of the transfer of the baton the incoming and outgoing runners are separated by 1 to 1.3m (distance of the arms length). There should be no forward or backward lean.

Many specialists believe in their analysis that the alternate upward sweep baton changing technique is the most effective and widely used method because it deviates less from the natural movement structure of sprinting than other changeover methods.

One of the most critical moments in the 4 x 100m relay is the changing of the baton. It requires a strict coordination of the speeds between the incoming and outgoing runners within the changeover zone. An optimum correlation of speeds is achieved by means of precisely calculated check marks, a vital aspect of relay running technique.

CHECK MARKS

The method of deciding the position of the check mark begins with the establishment of the exact spot for the baton passing (25 to 26m). It is suggested that this spot be marked with a cross. Next we determine the time the outgoing runner takes to cover 25m from a standing or modified crouch start (low start with the support of one hand and the head turned towards the incoming runner (t_1 = 3.24"). The time it takes for the incoming runner to cover the last 25m in the 75m section (2.25") in the 105m section (2.33") and in the 125m section (2.43" —i.e., V = 10.20") also are established.

Further, we calculate the differences between the 25m times of the incoming and outgoing runners ($t_1 — t_2 = t_3$) (3.24" — 2.25" = 0.99") and the average velocity (V) of the incoming runner over the last 25m (25m over 2.25" = 11.11m/sec). Finally, having determined the distance run by the incoming runner, an objective margin for the "start" is obtained:

(t_3 x V_{av} · = S of the start) (0.99" x 11.11 m/sec = 10.99m)

Consideration must be given here to the reaction time to moving objects. To this is added a selection reaction, as 6 to 8 sprinters in different lanes and moving at top speed hamper concentration. Investigations have established that most top-class athletes have a reaction time to moving objects of about 0.20". This means that running at a speed of 11.11m/sec. the incoming runner would have passed the check mark by 2.22m during the reaction time to moving objects of the outgoing runner (0.20"x 11.11 m/sec. = 2.25m). Consequently the outgoing runner will have to bring in the check mark to 8.77m, rather than use the calculated 10.99m.

We have established in our investigations three principles to be observed in the establishment of the check mark position:

1. The time of the reaction to moving objects of the sprinters must be taken into account.
2. The check mark used in training over a 75m distance is not adequate for competitive conditions. It enables the development of the interaction of the runners in the changeover zone (passing the baton, use of distance between the incoming and outgoing runners, reaction speed, etc.) but does not meet racing demands.
3. The check marks for competitive conditions should be established separately for the first (105m) and for the second and third (125m) legs with maximal intensity sprinting from start to finish.

COMPETITION PREPARATION

The Soviet national team prepared for the Seoul Olympic competition with twice a week training sessions (Tuesdays and Fridays), aiming mainly to perfect the technique of the interaction of the runners in the 20m changeover zone. In parallel, these training sessions also provided excellent workouts for the development of maximal speed capacities.

In order to resolve the set aims and objectives the following evaluations took place regularly:

- educational observations;
- electronic timing;
- video analysis of the baton changeovers.

In the beginning we studied the sprinting capacities of the team members in sections of 25m over the 75m distance. These indices were used in the calculations for the check marks for each pair according to the experimental method. In order to achieve perfection in the interaction of the runners in the changeover zone and pass the baton at the end of the zone (26th meter) we used a cross as a control marker.

"The final result in a 4 x 100m relay depends not only on the speed potential of the sprinters, but to a large extent on the technique of interaction between the runners in passing the baton within the 20m changeover zone."

The development procedures were based on the following:

- Baton changeovers in pairs within the 20m zone with a 60 to 75m run by the incoming athlete.
- Baton changeovers in pairs within the 20m zone in competition conditions. The incoming runners use 75 to 125m distances.
- Baton changeovers in pairs in which the athletes of all four legs run the full distance.
- Running of 4 x 50m, 4 x 100m and 4 x 150m relays in training.
- Closer to the competitions the preparations take place with the permanent line-up of the team members.

CONCLUSIONS

1. The following procedures may serve as criteria for evaluating the technical skills of the 4 x 100m relay for each pair of the runners:

   - Time of passing the baton in the 20m zone
   - Distance from the start of the running zone to the control marker
   - Differences in the time of entry into the changeover zone between the runners
   - Place of the baton transfer in the 20m zone.

2. It has been established that the running speed over the last 25m diminishes markedly when the running section of the incoming runner is increased from 75 to 125m. It is decisive to take this fact into consideration in the establishment of check marks for training and for competition.

3. Studies have shown that the individual running preparation of sprinters must be considered for each pair in the calculations to establish the check marks according to the following method:
$$t_1 - t_2 + t_3$$
$$t_3 \times V \text{ average} = S \text{ "check"}$$
$$\pm t \text{ reaction} \times V \text{ average} = \pm S_1$$
$$S \text{ "check"} \pm S_1 = S \text{ "check"}$$

4. The proposed method of calculating the check mark allows for the possibility of increasing significantly the distance of the check mark to ensure a stable changeover at the end of the 20m zone (26th meter) and a reliable interaction during the changeover.

Finally, the specifics of the relay sets severe demands on the starting speed, coordination capacities, speed endurance, motor reaction and psychological stability of sprinters. These qualities must be taken into account in the selection of relay teams and developed further in training.

4 x 100 METER RELAY RACING

by Jim Santos, USA

A former head coach at California State University, Hayward and a well-known clinician provides some good common-sense information on selection of personnel and baton passing technique.

Relay racing is the team event on the track and field program. It is fun for the participants and it pleases the crowd. The popularity of relays has perpetuated such great spectacles as the Drake Relays, Kansas Relays, Penn Relays, Coliseum Relays, to name a few. This popularity is deserved since a relay race offers spirited team competition and provides places for a large number of athletes who otherwise would not get the chance to participate. The grouping of relays permits competition for almost every type of athlete from the sprinter to the distance runner.

SELECTION OF PERSONNEL

This is a very tough job for the coach, perhaps the greatest responsibility he will face in preparing his relay treams for competition. The four members of a relay team usually manifest a wide range in characteristics and ability. Seldom are they equal in both ability and knowledge of racing tactics. Time and time again the deciding factor in losing or winning a sprint relay is the order in which relay members are put into competition. Here even more than in individual races, the adage "know thyself" must be supplemented by "know thy opponents". Coaches will find that careful and constant study of all related factors will pay important dividends.

I would suggest that the following points be considered in selecting your sprint relay personnel:

The Length of the Race

Since we are discussing the 4 x 100m relay, the personnel should and will be sprinters or hurdlers. In this race you should consider length of the race because it might be important to the success of the relay if one sprinter can run 95 or 115 yards quicker or with greater strength than another sprinter.

Which Athlete Runs Best When Behind

This is extremely important in the anchor leg of the sprint relay. There is not much chance to catch up in the sprint relay. Therefore, when a team gets behind, it is extremely important to have sprinters who can run well under this circumstance. Most sprint teams do not run well when they are behind. In many cases the runners lose their composure and blow the exchange. The second leg and anchor are important legs where consideration needs to be given to the sprinter who accelerates very quickly. Since both of these legs run their race on the straightaway, quick acceleration is important.

Which Athlete Runs Best When in the Lead

I would say this would be important on all legs of the sprint relay, especially the first leg. I feel that if you get the lead on the first or second leg you will win most sprint relays. This puts extreme pressure on the other teams. Most teams do not pass the baton well under pressure, especially when they can see they are behind. The quicker you can blow open the relay, the better your chances are of winning.

Who is the Fastest Starter and Best Starter

The best starter should take precedent over the fastest starter. Best starters will give a team the needed stability at the start of the race.

Who Are the Two Best Baton Handlers

In the exchange pass we use the second and third runners, each have two movements to execute, while the first and fourth runners each

121

perform but one movement. In this method it is necessary for the second and third sprinters to be the best baton handlers.

What Passing-Receiving Pairs Work Most Effectively Together

Adjustments are frequently required when athletes of varying heights, arm lengths, etc., are to be fitted into a smooth passing combination. Once we settle our combination in passing-receiving we do not change except for injuries. Then we hope that the alternate will do as well as the one he replaced.

The commonly accepted arrangement of a sprint team based on running still is 2,3,4,1. In this plan the most effective team member is placed in the anchor position. There are many other arrangements that may be used. A coach has to keep in mind at all times what is best for his team, or is he getting maximum effort from the athletes, with his arrangement of the relay. Another factor here that needs mentioning is the confidence between the passing and receiving pair.

You Should Consider the Ability of the Athletes to Run Into a Curve and Out of a Curve

In considering your curve runners you must consider who can start in the turn and who can run the full turn at full speed and at the same time prepare himself to handle the baton coming out of the turn. A sound procedure consists of carefully analyzing the four runners, determining the most effective order of carrying the baton, emphasizing judgment of pace so that each will run his respective leg at his optimum pace, and then retain his order throughout the season.

THE TECHNIQUE OF BATON PASSING

The introduction of the baton in relay racing has stimulated considerable investigation as to the best method of exchange and as a result there are a number of techniques used in passing the baton. There are five general styles of arm-hand position that most coaches use in the baton pass.

Definition of the Baton Pass

This is the exchange of the baton that takes place in a 20-meter zone with an additional 10-meter zone. There is only one accepted method of passing the baton in the sprint relay, and that is the so-called non-visual or blind pass.

There are seven factors a coach might consider when adopting a baton passing style for the sprint relay.

1. The distance of the relay race.
2. The mechanical efficiency of the exchange.
3. The adaptability of the style to the athletes.
4. The degree of certainty which a particular style provides.
5. The amount of free distance gained by the forward reach of the passer and the backward reach of the receiver.
6. The style providing optimum speed for both the receiver and the passer at the instant of exchange.
7. The distance of the receiver's target from the back line of the passing zone.

Variations in Baton Handling

Many coaches will say "receive with the right, pass with the left" or "pass the baton right to left" or "left to left" all the way. It is easier for the runner to receive the baton in his left hand because he is facing the inside of the track which obviously makes it simpler to extend the left hand. Also, most runners are right handed and can handle their right hand and arm better than the left for the pass. The pass that we use is right to left on all the exchanges, starting with the baton in the right hand.

Some teams omit the act of shifting the baton from left to right and each athlete carries the baton through his leg of the relay in the same hand in which it was originally received. The advantage of this plan is to save the cross-body arm motions by each of the last three athletes. It is a good method, but hard to teach and it has no distinct advantages.

The Baton Grasp

Frequently track coaches give little attention to the problem of holding the baton at the start of the race. The greatest hazard is dropping the baton or leaving it because of incorrect carriage or insecure grip. There are a number of grips that are used by the lead off man and all of them are good. A coach should take the following factors into consideration on starting a relay race with the baton:

1. A grip that is secure.
2. A position of the hand and baton that gives the starter comfort, relaxation and confidence.
3. The amount of exposed surface of the baton at the forward end will facilitate the passing to his teammate in the passing zone.

RESPONSIBILITIES

To be successful, an exchange of the baton requires certain definite accomplishments by both the passer and the receiver. An effective pass is defined as one in which the baton is exchanged when the two team members involved are running at an equal rate of speed, this rate being optimum for each, in the zone provided.

1. Responsibilities of the Passer (non-visual pass)
- He must judge and distribute his strength and efforts so as to reach his teammate in the shortest period of time. We believe that the responsibility for completing the exchange is upon the passer.
- The passer must make certain he can identify his teammate in the exchange zone and the lane. The best way is to get familiar with the lane before the race. Also, the passer can take into consideration the physical makeup of his teammate, plus he may use the color of the jersey of his teammate.
- His arm should be extended at the proper time, neither too early nor too late. Try to synchronize the arm movement of the passer with the arm movements of the receiver. The passer uses the command "hike" and the receiver extends his left arm back so that the hand is at a height approximately slightly above the hip. Once the passer gives the command "hike" his eyes never leave the extended left hand of the receiver until the exchange is made. Try to make the exchange 10-12 yards within the 20-meter zone. It gives both the passer and the receiver an opportunity to make any adjustments or correction before they are out of the zone.
- The passer is responsible for applying the correct amount of pressure to the baton in the exchange. He must make certain that his teammate can feel the baton and that he has a secure hold on it.
- The passer shouldn't anticipate the pass nor slow up to make the pass. If enough practice is spent working on the exchange both the passer and receiver will have the confidence that is necessary to get the job done in a highly skilled manner.

2. Responsibilities of the Receiver
- He must know that he is in the correct lane and he must know the exact location of both the back and front lines of the passing zone.
- The application of the foot drive and arm drive should be the same as in a start with the gun.
- The receiver must use good judgment as to the correct moment of initiating the get-away. In our system we use 7 strides, with a stride being about a yard in length. Of course this depends mainly on how many steps the runners feel they can handle between themselves. Also, it will depend on the condition of the track, wet, heavy or loose. The second the passer's front foot is above or coming down on the receiver's marker the receiver initiates his take-off with a slight pivot and pushes off.
- He should make certain he doesn't slow down or stop fearing that his teammate will not get there before he runs out the zone. He must remember that it's the passer's job to get the baton to him within the zone, and if he will discipline himself to run full speed for 6 or 7 strides before hearing the command "hike" he can expect the baton to touch his hand in most cases.
- A mark on the track in the zone is a recommended procedure to indicate that point when the hand is extended.

PHYSICAL CONDITIONING

All relay personnel should participate in a fall program to develop strength, endurance, speed and flexibility. This type of program has merit and will give the sprinter the basic foundation he needs to prepare himself for the indoor and especially outdoor program. This program consists of weight training, repetition work, and endurance work.

TECHNIQUE AS A PERFORMANCE FACTOR IN THE 4 x 100m RELAY

by Winfried Vonstein, West Germany

A German coach describes and evaluates the various baton exchange techniques and makes a case for the alternate changeover with the push passing method as the most efficient.

1. INTRODUCTION

The aim in the 4 x 100m relay is to carry the baton under competitive conditions as fast as possible around the track. This depends, not only on the fastest possible sprinting capacity of the team members, but also on the perfection of the changeover procedures. (Bauersfeld/Schroter 1986). Deciding technical elements allows teams of lower running capacity to compete successfully and make up for their shortcomings in sprinting ability through a correspondingly high technical level.

In spite of the significance of this, the technical literature contains comparatively few publications on relay racing. Most present basic exercises for the learning of the technique and the procedures of the baton change. The whole complex is still not sufficiently researched, its meaning still not appreciated.

The following text will shortly present and discuss the deciding elements in the technical factors of the relay.

Rules of the Race

The rules require that the baton is handed over from one runner to the next only within the 20m changeover zone. The changeover is completed when the baton is in the sole possession of the outgoing runner. The outgoing runners are allowed to start up to 10m outside the changeover area and can use additional markers (usually tape on synthetic tracks), denoted by Oberste (1979) as the "coincidence mark." This chosen mark designates "the point where the reaction movements should be started" (see Figure 1).

The outgoing runner observes the incoming partner, as well as the marker, and should, when the baton carrier crosses the coincident point, begin his acceleration. The coincidence mark is established by trial so that the baton carrying runner still reaches the fast starting outgoing runner to complete the changeover.

The term "coincidence mark" by Oberste (1979) is employed in the sense of clarity. The use of terms like the "starting mark" (Bauersfeld/Schroter 1986) can easily be confused with "starting line" (Bauersfeld/Schroter 1986) or the "starting point" (Jonath 1973) that signify the spot where the outgoing runner starts. The term "reaction mark" is also occasionally used (Loetz/Knebel 1982) (the common term in English is "check mark"—editor).

2. CHANGEOVER TECHNIQUE

The performance capacity of a relay team depends strongly on the level of the changeover procedures. The technique of the changeover comprises, according to Bauersfeld/Schroter (1987),

Figure 1: Diagram of the changeover (4 x 100m)

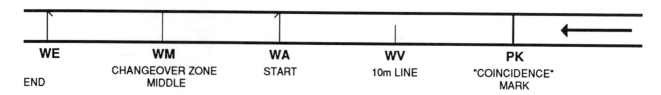

WE	WM	WA	WV	PK
END	CHANGEOVER ZONE MIDDLE	START	10m LINE	"COINCIDENCE" MARK

the following points.

- The type of the changeover
- The accuracy of the start and the acceleration of the outgoing runner
- The technique of baton passing
- The utilization of the changeover area.

Changeover Categories

We distinguish between three changeover categories:

- Outside changeover
- Inside changeover
- Alternate changeover.

The baton in the outside changeover is taken with the right (outside) hand, in the inside changeover with the left (inside) hand. The baton in both of these changeover categories is changed into the other hand after it has been received.

The alternate changeover, also known as the Frankfurt changeover (Jonath 1973), is made up from a combination of inside and outside changeovers. The first and the third are inside changeovers, the second is an outside changeover. The advantages of this type of changeover is that it requires no change of the baton from one hand into the other and reduces the risk of dropping the baton. The other advantage is in the shortest running distance, as the curve runners can run close to the inside lane line.

Oberste (1979) regarded as disadvantages of the alternate changeover the difficulties of an eventual correction of the grip on the baton, the larger curve of the incoming runner in the second changeover and the passing of the baton with the usually less skillful left hand in the second changeover.

According to my own experience, these disadvantages carry no significant weight. Taking and handing of the baton with the left hand is a question of regular training, the disadvantage of the larger running curve can be taken into consideration in the fixing of the check mark.

The alternate changeover is preferred because of the shorter running distance and the avoidance of the baton change from one hand into the other. All highly qualified relay teams employ the alternate changeover because of these obvious advantages.

Accuracy of the Start and Acceleration

Two essential demands are set for the outgoing runner:

a) He/she must achieve a maximal acceleration performance
b) the reaction to start must take place exactly at the coincidence point between the marker and the incoming runner.

This means that the outgoing runner must be in a position that allows, on one hand, the observation of the incoming runner and the check mark and, on the other hand, makes it possible to start with a maximal acceleration. The starting behavior in relay

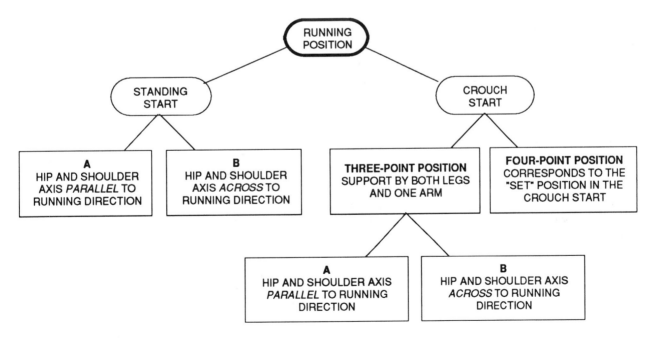

Figure 2: Starting positions of the outgoing runners in the relay (Oberste 1979)

125

racing is presented, according to Oberste (1976), in Figure 2.

The criteria of the acceleration capacity and the observation ability must be considered in the evaluation of the different starting procedures. It can be presumed that the three and four point positions have advantages, as far as balance and acceleration are concerned.

The most favorable observation conditions, according to Oberste (1979), result in the upright head position in the standing start (a variation in Figure 2). The necessary swing of the long axis of the body to start the acceleration can be developed in training so that there are no disadvantages.

The standing start position, because of the better observation, should definitely have priority for the less experienced runners. "The start from a crouch position is relatively difficult because the approach of the incoming runner can only be inaccurately judged." (Bauersfeld/Schroter 1986). The employment of a crouch start requires frequent training because of the difficulties of the head position for observation (Oberste 1979).

The accuracy and stability of the coincidence reaction is extremely important to reach high level relay performances and is frequently responsible for defective performances. For this reason I agree with Oberste that better observation conditions with an upright head position in the standing start must be given preference. Experienced athletes can, after sufficient training naturally switch to the crouch start and achieve with it possibilities for better acceleration.

"The outgoing runner must make every effort to reach the highest possible acceleration rate at the moment the incoming runner reaches the check mark (coincidence mark)" (Bauersfeld/Schroter 1986). This acceleration takes place as in normal sprinting. The arm of the outgoing runner is moved back to take the baton only after a short command called out by the incoming runner. The outgoing runner must even in this phase attempt not to slacken the tempo, while the incoming runner must maintain the speed.

It appears important here to point out that the runners who run in the straight don't necessarily have to keep to the outside of the lane. This can often impede the runners on the neighboring outside lane. Aiming to the middle of the lane leaves sufficient space for the changeover partners, saves a little of the running path and does not impede other runners.

Passing Technique

Two passing techniques are generally distinguished in the literature—the upward pass

and the downward pass. Oberste (1979) divides baton passing further, according to movement of the baton carrying arm, into swing and push techniques. As this is a more realistic terminology, it will be used here.

The baton in the swing technique is struck into the hand of the receiver in an arch. In the upward pass the baton is guided from below into the "area around the thumb" (Nett 1979), whereas in the downward technique the baton is guided from above into the palm of the extended arm of the receiving runner.

The baton in the push technique is pushed forward in a straight line into the horizontally placed hand of the extended arm of the receiver (Variation A, Figure 3). The variation B, although regarded by Oberste (1979) as potentially effective (vertical position of the receiver's hand), has in this author's opinion no practical advantage.

Oberste, who carefully evaluated the different passing techniques, came to the conclusion that the upward swing technique has disadvantages because of the difficulty in guiding the relatively large mass (extended arm). It is subject to considerable fluctuations. Further, the target area (receiver's hand) is relatively far away from the controlling organ (the eye) of the incoming runner. The negative influences of the extended arm/hand position of the receiver are quoted as a disadvantage in the downward swing technique.

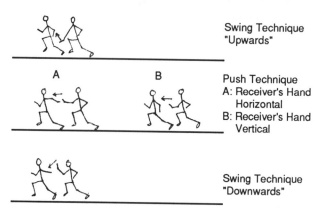

Figure 3: Different baton passing techniques (Oberste 1979)

The precision of the pass can shorten the "coupling phase" (Oberste 1979) and thereby increase the baton speed within the changeover zone. Improved guiding conditions make it possible to shorten the coupling phase in the push technique. The pushing movement, that involves in a sequence the shoulder, elbow and hand joints, allows for a better and more precise guidance of the baton. The movements of the incoming and outgoing runners are synchronized and it is not necessary to await the steady position of the receiver's hand.

Further advantages are shown in the studies by Schmidtke, who claims that underarm dominated target movements are more precise than overarm dominated movements, particularly when the target is at a level that corresponds to about 60 to 70% of the body height. In addition, Schmidtke points out that the striking rate in horizontally placed targets is higher than in vertically placed targets. Both occur in the push technique with an upward held baton. The push technique also makes it possible to gain distance through the widely extended arms of both changeover partners.

The decision in the evaluated changeover techniques falls in favor of the push technique. However, the arm position presented graphically by Oberste (Figure 3, variation A) can be regarded as poor in practice because running with an extended arm in the acceleration phase is extremely difficult for the outgoing runner. A relatively short extended arm phase is demanded in the push technique to avoid any hesitation in the acceleration.

The push technique, favored by this author, is presented in Figure 4. The baton is pushed forward in a straight line and pressed into the palm of the extended arm of the receiving runner. (A push-press movement).

Figure 4: The push technique favored by the author

Utilization of the Changeover Area

The rules require that the baton must always be passed within the 20m changeover zone. The outgoing runner is allowed to start from a line 10m outside the changeover area. It is therefore sensible, in order to achieve the highest possible baton speed, that the baton passing takes place well within the second half of the changeover zone. This allows the outgoing runner to reach the highest possible running speed. The baton speed depends on the running speed of the incoming runner up to the point of passing and is definitely higher than the speed of the accelerating receiver.

However, because of the possible risk factors in the passing of the baton directly at the end of the changeover area, it is advisable to execute the

start of the pass just after the middle line. The pass would in this case normally take place within two or three strides at around the third quarter of the changeover zone (approximately 15m). This is a calculated and necessary safety factor (Figure 5).

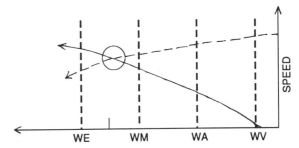

Figure 5: Speeds graph and the use of the changeover zone

3. SUMMARY

The performance technique of the relay covers the following points:

- the type of the changeover
- The acceleration run
- The technique of the baton passing
- the utilization of the changeover area.

The alternate changeover technique is favored because it allows a shorter running path and eliminates the change of the baton from one hand into the other while running.

As a precise start of the outgoing runner is of decisive significance, the standing start, because of its observation advantage, is preferable. Only experienced relay runners can switch to the crouch start for possible faster acceleration.

The push technique with an upright held baton is preferable from the known passing methods. It has the most favorable assumptions as far as an accurate control is concerned, the position of the hand of the receiver and a possible gain of distance.

A safety factor is calculated for the utilization of the changeover area, attempting to execute the actual pass of the baton at around the third quarter of the changeover area. Attempts to move closer to the end of the zone can take place only when both partners are extremely confident.

The presented factors clearly indicate that the sprint relay must be regarded as an event with its own technical elements that require objective development and training. This has to be taken into consideration in the planning for training for sprinters.

127